Elkan Niebohr, a larger than life, twenty-five carat bastard, head of the Excelsior Colonisation Corporation, was intent upon accomplishing, via very private enterprise, what his Government had reluctantly admitted they could not do, i.e., finance research which would lead to a warp-drive. For this, he planned to use Orphelin, one of the planets he owned, and its neighboring asteroid.

Needless to say, Niebohr, already a lot richer than the Government, did not have any philanthropic objective in mind. While normally untouched by any considerations of decency (one of his strongest assets) under conditions of stress, as when pursuing a mercantile end, Niebohr became actively ruthless. Since there was nothing small about the man—indeed, he was accustomed to wheel and deal with whole worlds rather than mere corporations—his activities were the concern not only of United Earth Government, but of its law-enforcement and defense agency, the Space Corps, and in particular, of Commander Bruce of the *Venturer Twelve*.

Whose unhappy—and very dangerous—job it was to discover what in hell Niebohr was really doing on Orphelin . . .

Also by Dan Morgan *and* John Kippax

A THUNDER OF STARS

SEED OF STARS

Available from Ballantine Books

THE
NEUTRAL
STARS

Dan Morgan *and* **John Kippax**

BALLANTINE BOOKS • NEW YORK
An Intext Publisher

BALLANTINE BOOKS, INC.
101 Fifth Avenue, New York, N.Y. 10003

The
Neutral
Stars

Chapter One

*There is a certain cowardice, a certain
weakness, rather, among respectable folk. Only
brigands are convinced—of what?—that they
must succeed. And so they do succeed.*

BAUDELAIRE

Gould was fully two minutes into his carefully prepared speech before he allowed himself to glance to
his left. Elkan Niebohr sat unmoving, a monolithic figure of indeterminate age, clothed in a dark grey business suit of natural silk. The great dome of his totally
bald head was poised slightly to one side in a listening
attitude, but the sandstone-textured face beneath,
with its heavy eyebrows and strong, hooked nose, had
the blank repose of a death mask. Only the hooded
eyes were alive, looking straight at Gould, watchful,
calculating, waiting. . .

Despite the fact that at least five other members of
the Excelsior Colonization Corporation board seated
around the huge circular table knew and approved of
what he was about to do, Gould felt a sudden chill of
loneliness. All the covert whisperings about Niebohr's

1

increasing age, the carefully hoarded scraps of evidence that the old man was losing his grip, the assurances of future loyalty and support—none of these held any meaning compared with the reality of the moment of truth that was rushing towards Gould. Intrigue in bug-proofed private rooms was one thing, but he had declared himself here in the arena, and now he must stand or fall by the power of his own words, words that by all logic must force commitment upon those members of the board who had, until now, remained on the fence. Their reticence so far had been due to fear of Niebohr, but once the first blood was drawn their hatred would overcome that fear. They would turn and rend him for the manner in which he had heaped indignity on them by the autocracy of his methods.

Only last month in a television interview he had said: "The Excelsior Corporation is *me!*" Such arrogance must be a sign of crumbling intellect. In the old days, when profits had been colossal and taxation low, eccentricity had been forgivable. But times were changing; the brigand image was no longer desirable. The colonization corporations of the future would be led by men with the minds of accountants—*men like Harold Gould.*

Having reminded himself of his destiny, Gould disengaged himself from Niebohr's gaze and plunged on: "In short, I and those who agree with me feel that the whole matter has been handled ineptly. If the campaign had been rightly pursued, the Senate should already be at least at the stage of debating concrete proposals about the arming of corporation ships. It is obvious that even within the present perimeter of colonized space the Corps is quite incapable of providing security. The Kepler* incident should be ample proof of the inadequacy of the Corps. But, apparently, no attempt has been made to capitalize on this or the other disasters involving the activities of the so-called Kilroys. . ."

Roth, the company secretary, intervened in his dry, precise, English-accented voice. "I should point out, Mr. Gould, that there is in existence a presidential directive to all media which requests that reference to such incidents should be minimal."

"Thank you, Mr. Roth." Gould nodded in the direction of the hunched figure of the company secretary. Roth was a Niebohr man right through to his cash register of a heart, but his interruption could not fail to reinforce the power of the arguments Gould had already planned. "I know about the directive, as no doubt do all the other members of the board, but thank you for the reminder. President Fong's directive indicates clearly his doubts about the ability of the Corps to handle the Kilroy menace. In plain words, he fears the panic that could be unleashed both here and in the colonies if the true situation were made clear.

"Yet he continues to deny colonization corporations the right to arm their ships at their own expense. The President has very strong ties with the Space Corps, but he is also an astute man. Have the facts of the matter not been put to him with sufficient clarity? I require a direct answer from the man who has for the last eighteen months been temporizing with excuses like: 'Leave it to me; this is my territory. I will handle it.' Just what steps, if any, have been taken to press our case in this matter?"

*Seed of Stars

Gould sat down, smoothing his damp palms on the thighs of his trousers, suddenly nervous now that his part in the proceedings was temporarily over. His arguments, as far as he had been able to frame them, were just and logical, but he was afraid. The board sat, the silence in the room thickening, damping even the background hum of the air-conditioning. All eyes turned towards Niebohr, waiting.

The old man's hooded eyes scanned the circular table slowly, a slight movement of a muscle at one corner of the thin mouth lending a hint of contempt to the gesture. Finally the eyes came to rest again on Gould, and without moving from his seat Niebohr spoke at last.

"Thank you, Mr. Gould," said the deep, careful voice. "We are all indebted to you for your oratory. Unfortunately your eloquence is exceeded only by your ignorance . . ."

Not far away to his right Gould heard a sharp intake of breath and guessed that Falangetti was panicking already. For himself he had expected nothing less. Niebohr was running true to form. Surely, if any further proof of the man's megalomania were needed. . .

". . . If a long and somewhat eventful life has taught me anything, it is that there are certain situations where even the proudest man does well to admit his limitations and seek the opinion of an expert," continued Niebohr. "Perhaps these are the beginnings of a new—and, some might say, overdue—humility."

There was a slight movement around the table, even the hint of a dry chuckle from one of Niebohr's more sycophantic supporters.

"Mr. Gould has been stupid enough to demand answers from me when he doesn't even know the corresponding questions. I think it is time we listened to someone who is qualified to assess the situation. I speak, of course, of my son-in-law Robert Prince, who as you all know pursued a distinguished career in the Space Corps for some years before resigning his commission and taking over command of the Excelsior Corporation fleet."

A tall, slimly-built man with thinning blond hair and blue eyes that were several shades lighter than his impeccable uniform, rose to his feet and nodded deferentially to Niebohr. "Thank you, Mr. Chairman. To begin with, it appears to be the general opinion that all that is needed to turn one of our ships—whether it be a freighter or a passenger vessel—into a dreadnought comparable with *Venturer Twelve*, is the installation of a few heavy-duty laser guns and a battery of launching tubes. Nothing could be further from the truth, I assure you. Our ships are purpose-built for the jobs they are doing at the moment. Apart from being costly, the physical modifications involved in providing them with an effective degree of fire-power would have serious side-effects.

"One of these would certainly be a lowering of the efficiency of these ships as far as their original purpose was concerned. In most cases this would mean that their operation was no longer economically sound."

Although there had obviously been an element of nepotism in Prince's initial appointment, any doubts about the ex-Corpsman's ability had been quickly dispelled by the manner in which he had reorganized the running of the Excelsior fleet. Gould knew that most of the other members of the board, like himself, had been forced to recognize that in Robert Prince they were faced by that comparative novelty, an honest man. Prince mainly held his own counsel, but when asked for his opinions on any subject he gave them without reserve. Despite his grudging respect for the man, Gould could not allow such a blanket assertion to go unchallenged.

"I'm sure that none of us here doubt your abilities, Commander Prince," Gould said carefully. "But are you saying that the ships of our fleet could not be modified?"

Prince turned to face Gould, his tanned face suddenly appearing at least ten years younger as his light blue eyes twinkled in an open smile. "Not if they are to continue to make a profit. And that, I understand, is the object of the exercise. As you so rightly point out, I am no accountant. As far as the financial side is concerned, I'm quite incapable of quoting figures and I shall not attempt to do so. If you have any such questions after I have given the technical explanations relating to my particular field, I would appreciate your directing them at Mr. Roth. We have talked, and I understand that he has prepared a detailed report on the cost-effectiveness of the possible modifications."

"Thank you, Commander," said Gould. He looked again at the silent, brooding figure of Niebohr, aware that the old man must have anticipated him at every point of his argument, might even welcome the challenge. He had no doubt that Prince's technical explanations would be unimpeachable, and Roth's figures correct beyond question. Gould savored the bitterness of defeat, made even more galling by the awareness that he had exposed, perhaps ruined, himself to no purpose.

"During my Corps service I had the pleasure, if that is the word, of serving for some months under Admiral Carter," continued Prince. "He was at that time supervising the construction of *Venturer Ten*. *Vee Ten* was a comparatively lightly armed vessel built mainly for speed, but even so, the generators and control equipment needed to make that armament function would have been sufficient to account for more than twenty-two percent of the payload of one of our Elkan-class freighters. I should also remind you of the maintenance and operational demands of such equipment. The crew strength of a ship so modified would need to be doubled at the very least, and the crew concerned would have to be trained in techniques and skills quite different from those at present demanded of the normal merchant spacer. Such highly trained personnel do not in fact exist outside the ranks of the Corps itself. To summarize, then, even if we were to obtain permission from the government to arm our ships, we would do so at the cost of losing a minimum of twenty percent in effective payload, plus at least a hundred percent increase in crew remuneration . . . *plus* the capital cost of the equipment itself. But more important than any of these aspects is the fact that we might well be undertaking such a ruinous burden to no purpose."

Prince paused, as if to assess the effect of his sudden paradox. Gould looked around the faces at the table. Only Niebohr and Roth remained outwardly unmoved. All the others registered shock to some degree, and there was considerable murmuring. He managed to catch Falangetti's eye at last, and as if responding to a certain guilt that he had sat silent while Gould had exposed himself earlier, the stocky Italian asked the obvious quesion.

"Commander Prince, would you please explain further?"

"With pleasure, Mr. Falangetti." Once again Prince

treated the members of the board to his boyish smile.
"Perhaps you, sir, can tell me the supposed purpose of
installing armament on corporation ships?"

Falangetti's fleshy face twitched nervously as if he
sensed some kind of trap, and he glanced across the
table at Gould, his dark eyes pleading for assistance.
Gould felt a twinge of rage that he could ever have
looked upon such a weak sister as a useful ally.
Falangetti was voluble in private, capable of manufac-
turing a fine quality in verbal ammunition, but he was
no damned good on the firing line.

"Commander Prince, let's *not* play guessing games,"
Gould said irascibly. "Everyone knows that the purpose of arming corporation ships is to enable them to
defend themselves and our colonies against attack by
the Kilroys—a task in which the Corps has been
consistently unsuccessful."

"I'm afraid I must agree with you on that last
point," said Prince, inclining his handsome, blond
head. "We have stumbled on evidence of Kilroy activities a number of times, and in each case this evidence has left us with the impression of a race so alien,
so utterly ruthless and inhuman, as to be quite beyond
our comprehension. We do not know what they look
like, where they come from, or what their purposes
are. But we can say with some certainty on the basis
of past experience that they have no regard whatso-
ever for the sanctity of human life. To call them
enemies, in the sense that I understand the word,
would be to credit them with anthropomorphic feelings which they may not possess. Perhaps it would be
more correct to suggest that towards the human race
they possess what would best be expressed as a
deadly indifference. Wherever our people cross their
path they are crushed and swept aside like insects,

obliterated by superior weapons, or used as laboratory animals in experiments whose purpose we can only begin to guess.* I speak of indifference because there is little doubt in my mind, or the minds of any of the Corps experts with whom I have discussed the subject, that should the Kilroys decide to destroy our solar system, the heart of United Earth itself, there would be very little we could do to defend ourselves under the present circumstances."

"Commander, are you seriously suggesting that the entire human race owes its survival to the fact that these aliens cannot be bothered to destroy us?" said Gould.

"Mr. Gould," said Prince calmly, "I have had the opportunity of studying the reports of the only definitely recorded encounter between a Corps ship and the Kilroys, also of talking at length with Commander Bruce himself on the subject. He assured me that, despite the fact that he was commanding the Corps' most modern fighting ship, he found himself quite incapable of preventing the destruction of Kepler III or of pursuing anything that could be defined as a meaningful attack against the alien ship. No weapon in his considerable arsenal was capable of piercing the Kilroy screens, and before he was able to make closer contact the alien ship disappeared. It did so, furthermore, without even bothering to make any reply to *Vee Twelve's* attack. Here again is the indifference I mentioned earlier. The purpose of the alien ship was the destruction of the Kepler planet, and once that was completed, whoever or whatever was in command saw no point in becoming involved in a conflict with *Vee Twelve*."

*Thunder of Stars

"You mean that, in effect, the Kilroys turned tail and ran, don't you, Commander?" suggested Gould.

"I only wish I could agree with you on that," said Prince. "I would find it easier to sleep nights. Commander Bruce's conclusion was that having completed its mission the alien ship returned to base as a matter of routine. At the most, if the Kilroys did regard the presence of *Vee Twelve* of any importance at all, Bruce considers that they may have allowed the ship to escape so that the story of the destruction of Kepler could be brought back to Earth as a warning."

Another member of the board, Rogers, who was sitting several places along on Niebohr's right, intervened.

"Commander Prince, is there *no* defense against these aliens?" His pale features were stricken with alarm.

"Under the present circumstances I would say that just about sums it up," replied Prince.

"The *present* circumstances?"

Prince nodded. "I'm surprised nobody has picked me up on my reference to the alien ship having *disappeared*. That seems to me to be a key factor. If Bruce had been able to move in closer, and at the same time to avoid being knocked out by the devastating power of the weapons which boiled the entire surface off Kepler III, he might have stood a greater chance of testing the alien's vulnerability to his own armament. However, before he could do just that—and I would remind you that Bruce has a reputation for swiftness in attack second to none—the Kilroy ship, in his words, 'shimmered into transparency and disappeared.' I have seen tapes of that particular episode, and I can assure you that it must have been an awe-inspiring experience. Those tapes have never been made public, of course; a presidential directive made sure of that. But as you can well imagine, they, and the accounts of eye-witnesses, have been the subject of exhaustive investigation in Corps circles. The general consensus of opinion is that the alien ships are powered by some kind of sub-space drive which enables them to cover immense distances almost instantaneously. In effect, the 'Space Warp' drive, which has for so long been the dream of theorists, now appears to be a reality. And it is this reality that makes even more believable the terrible possibility that the Kilroys could, if they wish, strike at the heart of United Earth and destroy it just as they destroyed Kepler III. They could perform such an act of genocide and disappear into sub-space again before any effective retaliation could be mounted against them."

"Then we are all doomed!" Rogers' voice was a wail.

"Not doomed—*on our guard,*" said Prince, the steel of his Corps training showing for the first time. "On our guard, and preparing for that day, if and when it comes. Not cowering and waiting for the blow to fall."

"Brave words, Commander," said Gould. "But as I understood it, you were the one who introduced a tone of hopelessness into the situation by your flat assertion that even if we were to beggar ourselves arming our fleet the effort would be useless."

"Because at the moment our ships would be nothing more than a flock of sitting ducks as far as any Kilroy attack was concerned," said Prince. "That situation, and not the matter of armament, should be our immediate concern. You may be aware of the existence of the Blue Mountain Project, which has been commanded by Admiral Carter for the past eighteen months. Carter was not lightly removed from his task of building *Venturer* ships, I can assure you. But the Corps is aware that there is no point in going on producing more and more ships which just don't have the necessary mobility in comparison with those of the Kilroys. The Blue Mountain Project is therefore concerned exclusively with research into the possibility of developing a Warp Drive."

"In other words, what you're saying to us is that there is little point in arming our own ships at this time because Corps ships equipped with the new drive will soon be capable of dealing with the Kilroy situation," said Gould.

"I'm afraid it isn't that simple," said Prince. "The 'new drive' doesn't even exist yet, except as a body of complex theory based on the mathematics of Koninburger. Added to this, there has been a clash of personalities, which I could have predicted from the outset for almost anyone dealing with an eccentric, easily offended genius like Koninburger. The upshot of this collision is that, in spite of pleas from the President himself, Koninburger has withdrawn from the Blue Mountain Project and holed up in his hunting lodge in the Black Forest. Blue Mountain is carrying on; Carter would be loathe to admit the indispensibility of anyone but himself, but it seems to me quite clear that without Koninburger's trail-blazing genius it may be a long time, if ever, before any positive results are achieved."

Gould frowned. It seemed to him that Prince had covered a great deal of territory without yet coming to the real point of his discourse. Obviously there *was* a point, but just what that might be. . .

"Thank you, Robert," said Niebohr, nodding in the direction of the younger man. "I think I can take it from there. Now, gentlemen. . ." The hooded eyes surveyed the members of the board one by one as Prince resumed his seat. "Commander Prince has explained to you just what a waste of money it would be to attempt to arm our fleet at the present time, even if we were capable of persuading the President that such a step was desirable. I am now going to propose that you make an open-ended investment in a project which some of you might earlier have considered wildly impractical and speculative. Clearly, a man like Koninburger does not lightly abandon work to which he has devoted most of his life, and which, should he succeed, would certainly gain him immortal fame and make him the potential savior of the entire human race. On the other hand, the very mention of the word 'Corps' is anathema to him at the present time. Bearing these facts in mind, two days ago I approached him on your behalf and offered him the backing of the Excelsior Corporation in establishing and running his own research program in the task of developing a Warp Drive. This backing will be free of financial limitations or conditions of any kind, other than a basic understanding that when such a drive is developed the patent will be assigned to the Excelsior Corporation in return for a guarantee of five percent royalty on all sales of the device."

Gould leapt to his feet, his face pale with emotion. "Mr. Niebohr, along with most of the other people around this table I have sat through Commander Prince's long discourse, increasingly mystified as to its ultimate purpose. I am mystified no longer. I intend no reflection on the sincerity of Commander Prince or on the truth of what he has said. But I do object to the manner in which you are trying to use those conclusions to justify this autocratic decision, which, in your own words, commits this corporation to an open-ended investment in a project that may never succeed in its objective."

"Thank you for your interruption, Mr. Gould," Niebohr said, deep-etched lines of contempt darkening at either side of the thin-lipped mouth. "If I had needed any reassurance about the correctness of my decision, your opposition would have provided it. There may be some people who think of you as a kind of Boy David for the apparently courageous way in which you have seen fit to oppose me here today. If they do so it is because they are, like yourself, in every way *small* men, pygmies whose brains cannot—or dare not—comprehend the larger issues involved. An open-ended investment—yes. . . But an open-ended potential in both profit and power for the Excelsior Corporation. With the Koninburger Drive, our ships will be able to travel at speeds that will make all existing methods of transportation derisory in their slowness. We shall be able to ship passengers and freight faster and further than any of our competitors, extending our sphere or influence even beyond the frontiers of known space. The Excelsior Corporation will become the most important organization in existence."

"But you're talking as if the whole thing were already a fait accompli!" protested Gould. "There *is* no Koninburger Drive. At the moment it is nothing more than an unrealized mass of ideas in the mind of a man who, although admittedly a genius, is not by any standard a specialist in practical applications."

"Gentlemen!" Niebohr raised one massive hand to point at Gould. "These are the squealings of a conservative, unadventurous mind. The future lies in the hands of the bold. I am an old man now. My reach may exceed my grasp, but there will be others who come after me who will see the realization of the dreams I dared to dream. And if any of you doubt the power of such dreams, let me remind you that thirty years ago this great Corporation whose destiny we guide existed only as an idea in the mind of a poor boy from humble origins who decided that for him there was no way to go but up. More than thirty-five years ago that boy went around to the offices of the money men—the merchant bankers, the wealthy speculators—talking, persuading, explaining, until finally he had the backing he needed to begin the realization of his great dream.

"But that was only a beginning. Planets were opened up one by one, money and work were poured into the building of a fleet of ships and the setting up of a number of colonies. A program of capital investment was established, so vast that the original backers began to express their nervousness, despite assurances that the apparently bottomless pit into which they were pouring their money would eventually become a source of profit. Some of them—I will not add to their remorse by naming the Judases—even went to the extent of selling their stock and pulling out. But Elkan Niebohr stood by his dream, worked and sweated to bring about its realization, refusing to be discouraged by fate or the wailings of pygmy minds."

In anyone else, the dropping into the use of the heroic third person when speaking of himself might have seemed a cheap trick, but even Gould found that he was impressed. One could doubt Niebohr's morals and his motives, but there was no denying the power of his physical presence and his oratory.

"Even in those days there were people who complained of Niebohr's autocratic methods, who failed to understand that you cannot steer a vehicle traveling at top speed along a bumpy road by the deliberations of a committee. One man must be at the controls, one man capable of sensing the hazards, of making split-second decisions and acting on them immediately. Orphelin Three was the result of such a decision, an almost blindfold bid made to the body then known as the Extra Solar Colonization Agency for sole rights to a newly discovered earth-type planet—a bid made on the basis of a very sketchy exploration report, because Elkan Niebohr had decided the time had come to play one of his hunches. . ."

Harold Gould listened, and marveled as he saw a living legend renewing itself before his eyes. He and most of the others around the boardroom table knew that there had been a great deal more to Niebohr's takeover of Orphelin Three than a mere hunch. There had never been any public scandal, both the Agency and Niebohr had made sure of that, but the Commander of the exploration ship in question had been retired prematurely from the service shortly afterwards, and it was rumored that the report that he had personally delivered to Niebohr was considerably more detailed than the one he submitted to his employers. Whether there was any truth in the rumor no one was likely at this stage to enquire, but there was no doubt of the fact that the retired captain had been employed in a nominally "advisory capacity" by the Excelsior Corporation at a salary more than ten times his service pay for the rest of his life.

"Orphelin Three, gentlemen," continued Niebohr, one arm outstretched, palm upwards as if holding the glowing jewel of a planet up for inspection. "A breakthrough in the history of colonization. A paradise planet, whose settlement was so organized that, instead of requiring many years of effort and investment before reaching the break-even point, it began to show a profit within a scant eighteen months. A planet where—thanks in part to our welfare policies, of course—the original population of colonists has now increased to almost five million. A planet of such fertility and lushness that its exports have increased year by year until at the present time they account for over twenty percent of the profits of this great Corporation. In that respect, I should add that we are expecting a considerable boost to this figure within the next couple of years, when the new fishery project gets under way. You may recall that at the time of first colonization the oceans, which cover eighty-two percent of the surface, were seeded with various earth-type fish—more particularly, varieties that were in danger of becoming extinct in the polluted seas of Earth. According to my preliminary reports from Doctor MacGuinness, the biologist who is at the moment conducting a detailed survey, the prospects are very good, especially with regard to salmon—a species which was at one time considered an expensive delicacy even by the more well-to-do people of Earth, but which has been so rigorously protected for the past seventy years that very few people living can ever have tasted its flesh. I need hardly add that our advertising department is already drafting for my approval a number of pilot campaigns designed to exploit this potential luxury market. With the background of such future planning, it seems to me that the stockholders of the Excelsior Corporation. . ."

Niebohr was in control.

Chapter Two

The man who does not seek to know himself in private meditation may find revelation in public disgrace.

MAHARISHI GUYNEHAH

Mario Falangetti's penthouse apartment was in the expensive Mamelin Heights section of Lake Cities. Perched high at the top of a soaring tower block, served by silently efficient anti-grav elevators, air conditioned and furnished in a luxurious Renaissance Modern style, it was a million miles away from the bustle and scurry of the thronging lower levels of Lake City, where Harold Gould had spent his childhood. A frosted glass clutched hard in his right hand, he looked out of the observation window, which covered one entire wall of the lounge, towards the great spangled phallus of the Excelsior Building two kilometers away.

"He used me—that crafty, conniving old swine!" Gould muttered.

Mario Falangetti, nearby, showed dark eyes full of concern. "No, Harry; how could you possibly have known? There's no point in blaming yourself."

"Because he's fooled better men than me in his time, is that it?" Gould turned to face his host, his lean features set in a grin of self-contempt. "Maybe so, but he sure nailed me. He led me by the nose right along the line. Niebohr, the big man."

"He *is* the big man," said Falangetti gently. "Whether you agree with him or not, that's something you've got to admit. Any time anyone questions that, all Niebohr has to do is point to the record. . ."

"Which he does."

"Not all the time," said Falangetti. "He's too clever to imagine that he can go on drawing on the credit of past achievements, even achievements as great as the Orphelin Three deal. He knows that whatever has gone before, there always has to be that carrot up ahead, the dream of bigger and better profits, of more and more power."

"Power for whom?" Gould said. "Nobody but Elkan Niebohr, and don't you kid yourself. Those sheep around that table, they just sit there on their fat butts and let him run things any way he likes. And when any one of them shows the slightest sign of getting out of line he gets slapped down, just like I was this afternoon. Remember me? I'm the bright young fellow who just got himself wiped out. It reminds me of something I read once in a book about the British Navy way back. There was this admiral who somehow got out of line, so they shot him. Some wit at the time said: 'to encourage the others.' That was my function. Nobody's going to stand up to Niebohr for a while, not after the way he demolished me." He downed the remains of his drink with a gulp and thrust the empty glass towards Falangetti. "Get me another one of those, for crissake."

Falangetti took the glass; he looked anxious. "Why

don't you call Mary and tell her you'll be staying the night here with us?"

"No—I told her I'd be home."

"Sure, but it's after eight already and its a two hundred mile run. Besides. . ."

"Besides, all I need right now is a drunk driving rap? The hell with that; I'll take my chances. Now, are you going to get me that drink, or do I have to go down to the cocktail lounge and buy one?"

"I suppose you figure I let you down," said Falangetti, moving towards the black-and-gold-decorated corner bar.

"Did I say that?"

"No, but. . ."

"Look, I was the bright boy with all the mouth. What was it the old bastard called me—the Boy David? So I blew it, because I was out of my class, and that's the end of it."

"But it isn't. We both know that," said Falangetti, returning with the drinks. "He won't fire you. You'll be shunted down some corporation back alley where you'll spend the rest of your life doing a rubber stamp job."

"Vice-president in charge of latrines, maybe? If I stick around." Gould took a stiff pull at the new drink and grimaced approvingly. "Now that really has bones in it. Keep the recipe."

"What do you mean, if you stick around?" pursued Falangetti.

"That's clear enough, isn't it? Look, Mario, I may be a pigmy in Niebohr's book, but I wouldn't have too much trouble getting a job with Solar."

"What about your contract?"

"Let Niebohr sue. There are one or two little ditties I'd take great pleasure in performing before an open court—like that load of pharmaceutical supplies that got shipped into Gavlan and landed Astral with a chronic drug addiction problem on their most promising planet. Then there was that trouble way back with the *Athena*. I was only a junior executive at the time, but I know where the copies of the manifest are for that trip. Not the one that was shown at the court of inquiry—the *real* one."

"What good would it do anyone to rake up that kind of dirt?" said Falangetti, his pale forehead furrowed in a worried frown.

"None at all," said Gould, grinning. "And I'm sure it will never come to that. I was just saying what *could* happen."

"Look, things may not really be that bad," said Falangetti with a forced air of cheerfulness. "Once Prince takes over there are bound to be a lot of changes."

"Prince?" Gould snorted his derision. "Did you fall for that 'handing on of the torch of progress' routine too? I tell you this, that old man isn't going to hand *anything* on until they pry it from his dead fingers—and he's going to live for quite a while yet. Prince is a fine fellow, all right, but he's nothing but a babe in arms as far as Niebohr is concerned. He may or may not succeed to the presidency when Niebohr finally dies, but for the time being he's just a piece of democratic window-dressing to keep the board and the stockholders happy while the old man continues to run things in his same old dictatorial way. I tell you another thing. . ."

He stopped speaking as Toyo, Falangetti's Japanese wife, came into the room. Tiny, and cute as a button in a jade green kimono, she approached the men, smiling.

"Dinner in twenty minutes," she said. "Won't you change your mind and stay, Harold?"

Gould shook his head regretfully. "You know that under normal circumstances I could never resist your *tempura*, but tonight I promised Mary I'd make it home." He glanced at his wrist watch. "In fact, I should have been on my way ten minutes ago."

"All right, I'll let you go, provided you promise that both of you will come over one night next week— say, Wednesday?"

"It's a date," said Gould. "Sorry to drink and run, but that's the way it has to be."

Pausing to give Toyo a peck on the cheek, he hurried out into the hallway. Falangetti followed on behind, his round face troubled.

"Look, Harold, I can't help having this feeling that I've let you down in some way. Maybe we can get together again tomorrow and figure something out?"

"Forget it, Mario," Gould said, with every appearance of cheerfulness. "This is one situation that I shall have to figure out for myself. Thanks anyway." He shook hands and walked quickly out along the corridor towards the elevators.

On the way down to fiftieth level, alone and robbed of the rattle of his own brave talk, his spirits began to sink. A great deal of what he had said to Falangetti had been nothing more than whistling in the dark. The boast about the exposures he would make if he were brought to court in a breach of contract action were nothing more than that, he knew. Niebohr would go to any lengths at all to prevent such a thing from happening.

Walking out of the elevator toward his parked fly-car, Gould was already coming to the humiliating conclusion that the safest and most sensible thing he could do would be to relax and accept whatever demotion or railroading Niebohr cared to hand out to him, to sing small and hope, as Falangetti had suggested, that things might be slightly different when Prince finally took over.

Fine. . . But how was he going to explain such a sudden check in his upward progress within the corporation to Mary? She was very sensitive to such things, and she took a real pride in his advancement that had nothing to do with the financial aspect of the matter.

The flycar motor purred into life and he lifted the vehicle swiftly from the park, heading for the northbound five hundred meter lane. Five minutes later, having reached his perimeter checkpoint, he switched over to automatic and adjusted his seat to the reclining position.

He lay back, looking up at the vastness of the stars through the transpex canopy, a sight that normally never failed to bring with it a comforting sense of order, of a universe planned and created for a purpose. But tonight his mind kept drifting back to the events of the day, to the boardroom, to the hopelessness of his situation, and the expression on Niebohr's cruel death-mask of a face.

That face seemed to fill his consciousness, the stars themselves flowing and coalescing until he found himself staring up into its glowing image—the hooded eyes, the great dome of the head—looking down at him, the thin mouth twisted in an evil, gloating grin.

A sudden change in the note of the flycar's engine jerked him back into full consciousness and the realization that he had been dreaming.

Bringing his seat forward, he switched the controls back to manual and began to nurse the faltering engine. For some reason control must have diverted him to another lane, because the altimeter showed a reading of eight hundred meters. Looking downwards, he saw that he was passing over the craggy mountainous country of the ridge some twenty kilometers south of his home. Not far, if he could only keep the craft in the air. Failing that, if he had to bail out, a State Police patrol should pick him up within a few minutes by tracking the emergency beacon on his anti-grav chute.

Two minutes later it became manifestly clear that his efforts with the controls were having little effect, as the engine died completely and the car began to lose height rapidly. Too bad for the insurance company. There was no sense in hanging around any longer.

Slipping on the a/g harness, Harold Gould pressed the lever that blew the canopy of the flycar. The wind hit him like a club, knocking the breath from his body for a moment. He recovered and dived out into the night, the craggy landscape whirling dizzily below him as he pressed the activating button on his chute, bracing himself for the sudden, checking effect as the a/g generator burst into life and slowed his fall.

He was still waiting at a hundred meters. Then he began to scream. . . .

Chapter Three

The discovery of a new dish does more for human happiness than the discovery of a new star.

BRILLAT-SAVARIN

Angus Alexander MacGuinness, M.Sc., B.Sc., M.B. (Edinburgh), carefully removed the last of the sizzling, three-centimeter-thick salmon steaks from the frying pan and placed them on the hot plate inside the portable cooker. Then he picked up the basin containing the prepared mixture of cream, chopped chives, pepper, salt and herbs with his left hand and poured it into the pan, stirring energetically with his right to combine the mixture with the residual juices and oil remaining in the pan after the cooking of the fish. A savory, palate-tickling aroma rose from the mixture, filling the small geodetic dome hut, bringing looks of anticipation and approval to the faces of his audience, two well-built, greying men apparently in their mid-forties.

"Gentlemen, you are privileged to be present at the creation—or I should say, rather, the re-creation—of a culinary masterpiece," said MacGuinness. "A dish that was first prepared by the great Donald MacGuinness when he was chef to her late Majesty Queen Victoria. The recipe has been handed down through the male line of the MacGuinness clan, remaining a closely guarded secret despite the continued importunings of Sassenach gourmets, for nigh on three hundred years. Furthermore, it has been tasted by no one on Earth for more than seventy years because of the lack of that noble fish which is its main ingredient. Now, by the grace of God and the fertility of this paradise planet, Orphelin Three, I present for your delight Saumon MacGuinness!"

The eminent biologist removed the dish containing the salmon steaks from the hot plate and placed it in the middle of the table. He smothered it in the steaming aromatic sauce, then stood back, beaming at the others through his immense proliferation of black hair, beard and sidewhiskers.

"Sure looks good, Professor," said Bill Emery, his weatherbeaten face breaking into a grin.

"Smells kind of nice too," added Alan Emery, who looked exactly like a slightly older version of Bill, with the same tight-curling hair, except that it was several shades nearer white, and the same broad, open features, even more deeply weathered, with a network of wrinkles.

"Aye, lads, but the proof of the pudding is in the eating thereof, as my old daddy used to say," said MacGuinness, producing a fish slice and a large spoon. His movements gained a theatrically exaggerated flourish, no doubt inherited from the great Donald along with the recipe, as he proceeded to serve the portions, each with its carefully measured amount of sauce. "The two crucial *sine qua nons* of the masterpiece lie at either end of its creation, you would do well to note. In the first place, the steaks must be flamed in a good quality whiskey before cooking—and secondly, when the dish is finally ready, it must be served on hot, not warm and *certainly* not cold, plates. Failure in either of these matters can mean disaster."

The serving and his lecture on *haute cuisine* completed simultaneously, MacGuinness motioned his two companions to sit down and begin the meal. As a man who, despite his deceptively stringy build, had a firm grip on his priorities, MacGuinness attacked his portion, eating with a single-minded devotion that left no room for mere conversation.

Some ten minutes later, having wiped what remained of the sauce from his plate with a slice of bread, he sat back with a satisfied sigh. "No' so bad, considering I've had very little opportunity for practice," he said, extracting a thin cigar from one pocket of his safari jacket. The potentially dangerous operation of lighting the cigar, embedded as it was in the fire hazard of his bushy, free-sprouting black whiskers, was a masterpiece of control, watched by his companions with something like awe.

"Professor, I reckon you're a genius," said Alan Emery. "This calls for a toast." He picked up a bottle that was half full of light amber liquid and bore the label: Bell's Original Scotch Whiskey.

Bill Amery frowned. "You know we're not used to that stuff, Alan. Just pour one for the Professor, and give my glass a miss."

"Suit yourself," Alan said. "But I'm having another." He poured for himself and MacGuinness.

The biologist savored his drink and chuckled. "Ha!

I remember that supercargo's face when I brought fifty cases of Bell's for my own personal use. 'If the bloody whiskey doesn't go,' I said, 'then I don't, and you'll have to sort it out with Elkan Niebohr.' By the way, 'personal' does extend to my friends. And even though you're not used to it yet, I'm sure you'll soon develop a tolerance."

"I'll second that," said Alan. "But I think that the main toast of the evening should be to Donald MacGuinness. Come on, Bill—just this once."

Bill shrugged. "All right, but only a small one." He picked up the bottle. "I still think this stuff could get a hold on a fellow, and its sure a great tongue loosener."

"So what does that matter?" grinned Alan, his eyes already slightly glassy. "We're all friends here, aren't we?"

The toast was drunk with enthusiasm and was swiftly followed by others to Queen Victoria, Bonnie Scotland, all the Emerys past and present, and us (wha's like us?) in a glowing flood of alcoholic bonhomie that took them through the remains of the original bottle and well down a second.

MacGuinness remained remarkably composed, seated bolt upright in his chair, the only outward sign of his inebriation being an increasing tendency to hold forth in a manner that could only be described as portentous. Although his audience had long since been declared honorary MacGuinnesses, the fact was that they had not been born with the tolerance for usquebaugh possessed by true members of the clan. Bill had already retired to his cot in the corner. Alan was still nominally awake, a cherubic grin on his broad weatherbeaten face, but he was clearly feeling very little pain.

"Ye see, lads," said MacGuinness, pausing in the perilous operation of lighting yet another cigar. "This planet of Orphelin Three is really something a great deal more special than anyone guessed in the first instance. A paradise planet, manifestly—the way your colony has thrived is ample proof of that. But what are the factors that combine to make this paradise a fact? I doubt whether anyone has ever taken the time out to inquire really closely. The Excelsior Corporation has been happy with its profits, and you people have been fully occupied in living your own lives and working—which is as it should be.

"The scientific mind, however, looks rather more deeply into such matters. As you already know, the original colonization ship carried, in addition to its usual complement of passengers, supplies, seed, and domestic livestock, the beginnings of an interesting ecological experiment. Based on the fact that eighty-two percent of Orphelin's surface is covered by water, it was assumed that the colony as it grew would depend more and more for sustenance on the products of the oceans. Strangely enough, the first exploration parties found the local varieties of fish, although technically edible, mainly bony and tasteless. This being so, it was decided to seed the oceans with quantities of fry and spawn of the more popular Earth food fishes, including the cod, herring, mackerel, and salmon. However, despite its growth, the entire colonial population is still living on the main continent of Tantaron, where the agricultural yield is so high that even a minimum of effort produces a substantial surplus of food. Supplementary sources such as fisheries have therefore remained unnecessary and, until this time, uninvestigated. Now, in his infinite wisdom the President of Excelsior Corporation, Elkan Niebohr, has sent his obedient servant, Angus Alexander MacGuinness, to investigate the results of that experiment begun over twenty years ago. Mr. Niebohr, I might add, is not paying my vast salary (and expenses) in order to satisfy any scientific curiosity on his part, but, as is his custom, in pursuit of his holy and unceasing quest for the fast credit.

"Mr. Niebohr has the idea that even though you Orphelins, living as you do in the lap of luxury—one might even say God's Pocket—scorn the products of your own oceans in favor of T-bone steaks and succulent hog meat, the less fortunate inhabitants of polluted Earth and the comparatively barren planets of the Sol system will welcome the import of quick-frozen fresh fish. You fortunate mortals may not be aware that synthetic protein constitutes more than eighty percent of the humdrum diet of even the comparatively affluent classes on Earth. I will not bore you with the horrors of the soyburger and the simulated algal steak. Suffice it to say that Mr. Niebohr—an odious person who boasts that, while he may not always be right, he is *never* wrong—once again appears to have backed a winner.

"Without exception, the Earth-type fish seem to have thrived in their new environment—as the noble salmon of our recent acquaintance bears witness. Despite a certain culling by local predators—a matter to which we must give our attention shortly—this species has established extensive breeding grounds in the creeks and pools of the islands to such an extent that there has been a veritable population explosion. Apart from the obvious factors such as an equable climate and an abundance of natural food, my researches indicate that this is due to what I can only describe as an evolutionary leap in the development of the species. This has brought about such an accelerated rate of maturation and growth that an Orphelin-reared salmon becomes adult at the age of eighteen months and begins breeding correspondingly earlier. Thus, the whole life-cycle of the fish appears to be speeded up to something like seven times its Earth equivalent. From the commercial fishery point of view this is an obvious advantage, and although I do not like to jump to conclusions, I would say that even at a conservative estimate there is no reason why Orphelin should not export at least a hundred thousand tons of salmon alone each year, once the fishery is in full operation. This should gladden even the flinty heart of Mr. Niebohr, when he receives the report which I have today transmitted to Josiahtown for relay to Excelsior headquarters back on Earth. It should also be pretty welcome news to yourselves, because the experience you are gaining with me on this trip, plus my recommendations, should make it quite certain that the two of you automatically obtain high posts in the organization of the new industry. In many respects I envy you. A resident job here on Orphelin would suit me fine, but my sabbatical ends in a few months and I shall have to return to the treadmill of lecturing a horde of stupid, not to mention ungrateful and inattentive students. There is something so refreshing about working in the field, getting to grips once again with—"

MacGuinness's peroration was brought to a halt by the sound of a deep and unmistakable snore. He looked across with some severity to see that Alan Emery was slumped forward over the table, his head cradled in his hands.

"Sassenachs!" murmured MacGuinness, surveying his sleeping audience. "Ah, what can ye expect?" He rose and proceeded out of the hut with solemn, stiff-gaited inebriety to contemplate the night sky of Orphelin Three.

Chapter Four

> *Thou shalt not kill: but need'st not strive officiously to keep alive.*
>
> CLOUGH

"State Police Headquarters announced this afternoon that after over twenty-four hours of searching, one of their patrols had finally succeeded in locating the body of Harold Gould in a canyon some five kilometers from the wreck of his flycar. Preliminary investigations indicate that Mr. Gould, who was on his way to his mountainside home in Atikokan, was killed as a result of a power-pack failure in his a/g chute belt. One of the younger members of the board of the Excelsior Colonization Corporation, Mr. Gould leaves a wife, Mary, and two children aged three and seven years. After an early career in accountancy he moved. . ."

The voice and image of the newscaster faded abruptly as Elkan punched the cutoff button. He had little taste for obituaries, even those of his enemies.

"What make of chute was he using?" he asked, turning to his companion, a square-featured man whose dark business suit fitted him like a uniform.

"Safetee Aid," said Kurt Wernher.

"Produced by a subsidiary of Solar Corporation, if I'm not mistaken?"

"That is correct, sir."

"Good! Excellent!" Niebohr's heavy features creased in one of his infrequent smiles as he punched the memo button on his desk. "Legal department—mount a suit on behalf of Mrs. Mary Gould, claiming two million credits for criminal negligence connected with the failure of her husband's Safetee Aid a/g chute. And. . .they're bound to come up with an offer, but we don't want any out-of-court settlement. I want this thing played up big, the full three-ring circus. . ." He pressed the hold button and turned to Wernher. "What about the wife—is she a looker?"

"On the thin side, reddish hair and good legs," said Wernher.

"I'm not asking you to lay the bitch," snapped Niebohr. "All I want to know is will she make a good showing in court?"

"Used to be a TV actress. I'd say she was a natural for the widow's weeds ploy."

"Fine! Get her up to my office first thing tomorrow morning."

"Right. What about the kids?"

Niebohr grimaced. "Keep them on ice for later; we'll gauge momma's potential first." He released the hold button. "Public Relations: Prepare a draft statement for release to all media on my behalf about the death of Harold Gould. Untimely demise. . .great future. . .one of our brightest young executives—you know the kind of crap. And check with Legal on a reference to the Safetee Aid a/g chute responsible for his death."

He switched the memo off and turned once again to Wernher.

"You did a good job, Kurt, as usual."

"Thank you, sir. I do my best." The big man's heels clicked faintly as he bent his barrel-chested body forward in a slight bow.

"You do indeed, Kurt, because you know that I would be satisfied with nothing less," said Niebohr, scanning the other's square features and detecting, with those invisible antennae of empathy that had served him so well in the past, a hint of unease. "There was something else?"

Wernher colored slightly. "Your speech at the board meeting yesterday. . ."

"Which part of it?"

"The reference to the fact that Commander Prince is to take over presidency of the corporation. I was wondering. . ."

Niebohr's monolithic form shook briefly in a soundless chuckle. "You're thinking perhaps that our Honest Bob may have no use for your particular specialties?"

"I must admit that thoughts along that line had occurred to me," admitted Wernher. "From my experience of the Commander, it seems that his operating methods may be somewhat different from your own."

"Good! Good!" Niebohr grunted with apparent pleasure.

"Sir?"

"My dear Kurt, if *you* were convinced then I need have no fears of scepticism from any of those dimwits on the board. Apart from the overly ambitious Mr. Gould, who I believe fancied himself for the post, most of them will be completely happy under the new régime—provided the profit percentages keep up.

And Prince's reputation for probity will add a new luster and respectability to the Excelsior image."

"Even so, sir. The idea of your retirement. . ."

"Retirement, for God's sake! What would I retire *to?*" exclaimed Niebohr. "I named my successor, but I made no mention of the date of my abdication. It should be obvious to anyone that even Robert Prince could hardly be expected to step into my shoes without a considerable period as a trainee—a period that will not be all roses for the person concerned, I assure you. Do I make myself clear?"

"But the time will come, much as I personally will regret it—"

"You lying bastard, Kurt. You never regretted anything in your whole life, except perhaps the fact that my little Elsa preferred the screwing she got from Prince to your brand."

"Did she?" A hint of anger lurked in Wernher's cold grey eyes.

"I didn't push her into it, if that's what you're thinking. She made her own choice, freely, without any deference to me."

"But nevertheless you approved."

"I didn't *disapprove*, certainly," said Niebohr. "The good Commander and his spotless Corps image could not fail to be an asset to us. But it wouldn't have made any difference to me if he'd been a bum, so long as he made Elsa happy."

Elsa was the youngest of the three children born to him by his wife Belle, and the only one who had not been a disappointment to him. The other two were both boys. Elkan Junior, the eldest, was a priest of the United Christian Church, with a parish in the part of the Federated States of Africa that had once been known as South Africa. A born agitator with a chip on his shoulder from the first day he began to talk, young Elkan had been in and out of jail a dozen times because of his insistent campaigning for the rights of the white minority. A big man, with a younger version of his father's impressive ugliness, he was a disappointment to Niebohr, and the two of them had not met since Belle's funeral some ten years earlier.

Alvin, the younger son, seemed to have inherited all his mother's weaknesses, to which he added quite a number of his own. Shiftless, idle and uneducable, but with a certain sly charm, he had committed most of the crimes in the book by the age of fifteen and ruined his health by constant and varied debauchery by the time he was twenty-one. At the moment he was under deep sedation treatment for Shoot addiction, but the prognosis of the doctors was that his burned-out nervous system would fit him for little more than a vegetable existence when he finally came out of it.

Only in Elsa had the father seen his hopes for a worthy child fulfilled. She had inherited her mother's slimness and dark good looks and her father's brains. In his rare moments of self-derision Niebohr thanked whatever gods may be that it had not been the other way around. She was a young lioness, handsome, proud and ruthless, with none of that weakness that had finally driven Belle to suicide. At last, and too late, in his own daughter Niebohr recognized the kind of woman who would be capable of becoming his partner and equal—a quick brain, with all his own skills in the art of using people, plus several more against which his age and sex precluded competition. And yet he had made no attempt to discipline her, or to force upon her the idea that she might eventually become his successor, but gave her the freedom that she would have taken anyway to lead her own life in the way she chose.

She chose, as he had come to understand over the past four or five years, the woman's way—the infinitely more subtle, self-effacing method of dominating her environment and associates, known to her sex over the ages, based on the principle that men and women were not equals, but *different*. Watching Elsa, Niebohr had come to realize fully for the first time that a clever woman aware of and capable of using those differences could always defeat any man. He himself had been a willing and amused victim on many occasions—for him there was some novelty in being dominated. Belle had been beautiful, but weak—and his own nature was such that this left him with no alternative but to destroy her with a million psychic pressures.

Elsa, on the other hand, was strong and calculating, aware of and capable of using all her considerable weaponry to attain her own ends. In the early experimental days he had wondered if she was not perhaps a trifle too promiscuous for even these uninhibited times, but that phase had soon passed, and she began to indulge her appetites with a great deal more discretion and calculation. Wernher, for instance, had been an obvious target for her attention. The fact that he was a reasonably attractive, virile male had been secondary to the consideration that his close association with her father, and his particular talent for organizing the discreet removal of human obstacles, would make him a useful acquisition. And once Elsa acquired a man, even though she never laid him again he remained tied to her by some invisible thread that very few had managed to break. It was a kind of relationship that Niebohr, who satisfied his occasional

sexual urgings with the impersonality of a man piss-
ing against a wall, found difficult to understand, but
he was forced to recognize its existence. He knew that
Wernher and a hundred other men would still come
running to act as her willing slaves if she beckoned.
As for Robert Prince, her husband, he had probably
been the most useful acquisition of all to date, and
he promised to be even more so in the future.

Niebohr was not fond of contemplating the prospect
of his own eventual death, but the concept was at
least made slightly more bearable by the confident assumption that while the reins of power would apparently be passed to Prince, they would in reality
be wielded by his true heir, Elsa.

Niebohr came out of his reverie. "Don't worry about
any succession, Kurt," he said. "Caesar will show himself mighty at Philippi."

"Shakespeare," Wernher said, *"Julius Caesar.*
Goethe couldn't have said it better."

Chapter Five

Commander Thomas Winford Bruce, Captain of Corps ship *Venturer Twelve*, sat resplendent in his full-dress uniform at the controls of the two-seater fly-car as it soared over the northern foothills of the Appalachian Mountains. It was early evening, and the fascinating pattern of the ground beneath was sharpened and given extra dimension by the angle of the light cast by the setting sun. He glanced appreciatively at his companion.

"I'm glad you decided to come as a woman," he said.

Helen Lindstrom smiled. Beneath a white fur cape she was wearing a plain white gown that was exactly right for the blonde opulence of her beauty. She wore no jewelry except for a blue-star clasp at her right shoulder, and that was no piece of mere display but the symbol of a Corps citation for gallantry. Bruce noticed the touch and was amused at the way she had kept the letter of Regulations and told the spirit to go to hell. Lindstrom, his second-in-command aboard *Venturer Twelve,* was a fine officer, but she was also one hundred percent woman, as he had good cause to remember. She had been *his* woman once, until he had been forced into the decision that their continued relationship was not compatible with their duty to the Corps. It had been a hard decision to make, and an even harder one to maintain. There were times when. . . He thrust the dangerous train of thought to one side and said: "Does that gown have any special message for anybody?"

She half-turned her head and gave him a cool stare from her deep-blue eyes. "What do you think?" She opened the cape, her lips twitching with amusement.

He scanned the slashing décolletage. "I'd say that was a loud and clear challenge to any male member of the company."

"Maybe. . . But I don't think of it that way," she said.

"For the women?" His grey-speckled reddish eyebrows raised slightly.

"Naturally. Who else do women dress for?"

"Translation please."

"Very good sir." She flashed him a cheekily sloppy salute. "It says, quote: 'I don't need to wear a bra; if you do, then hard luck, mate.'"

Bruce threw back his head and laughed. "I can think of a number of sagging matrons who are just going to love that."

"The monastic life holds some compensations," she said, her eyes holding his own for a moment longer than necessary. At last he deliberately looked away and fussed with the controls. They flew on through the deepening twilight in silence for several minutes until Bruce spoke again.

"This shindig tonight—I still haven't figured Henry Fong's angle."

"Whatever made you think you're intended to?" said Helen. "In any case, he's only making the presentation. The award itself was voted on by the members of the Colonization Development Commission."

"And who do you think pulls the strings?"

"Are you suggesting that Fong has ulterior motives?" asked Helen mischievously.

Bruce appeared not to notice. His brooding face beneath the carefully trimmed thatch of silver-flecked red hair remained serious. "I can't think of any other reason. Do you really think that Niebohr is ripe for canonization?"

"There's no denying his services to the cause of colonial expansion. The Orphelin project alone. . ."

"Bullshit!" Bruce snapped. "Orphelin Three is a big deal, sure, but it was founded by conniving and wheeler-dealing, to put it at its kindest. You're not going to tell me that Niebohr didn't buy that exploration ship captain. How he ever got away with it I'll never understand. He certainly wouldn't today."

"You've got to give the old bastard credit where credit's due," Helen said.

"If we're bandying clichés, I'd prefer 'the Devil his due.' "

"You're prejudiced."

"Too bloody right I am, and don't you forget it!" Bruce said, with some heat. "When I think of what he tried to do to us over the *Athena** affair."

Thunder of Stars

"Water under the bridge. That was years ago."

"Tell that to the five hundred men, women and children who died."

Helen sighed. "You're in a real party mood this evening."

"It may be a party to you, honey child. But to me it's just an assignment."

"Why don't you just relax for once? You might find yourself having a good time."

He looked at her, his handsome features still stern. "Sometimes I worry about you. Like, however did you get the idea that you're *supposed* to have a good time at this kind of affair?"

"Oh, come off it, Tom! You're looking forward to seeing your old chum Bob Prince for the first time in two years. It will be 'do you remember when. . .?' and 'Happy days at dear old Sandpoint' all the way."

"I wonder. . ." Bruce said thoughtfully.

"You're not still sore at him for opting out and joining the commercial sector, are you?"

Bruce shrugged. "Why should I be—it's his life."

"You mean his *wife*, don't you? After all, he could hardly turn down the kind of opportunities marrying her must have opened up for him. In fact, some would say that was putting the cart before the horse. . ."

"Now you're being bitchy," Bruce said. "Bob Prince is one of the straightest guys I ever knew."

"But he did manage to sell himself dearly, you will admit that. Elsa's no mean catch, even if she does have legs like a brace of Mark IV Engelschaft missiles."

Bruce looked at her, a touch of humor kindling in his green eyes. "Wow! When you put on the female thing it really goes down to the bone marrow, doesn't it? Just for your information, strange as it may seem considering her parentage, Elsa Niebohr is a pretty good-looking femme. I wouldn't kick her out of bed myself."

"Now steady on there, Commander," Helen said, grinning. "The old chums routine doesn't go that far —even at Sandpoint. Mind you, I understand that she played the field pretty thoroughly before they committed marriage."

"Let's leave it there, shall we?" said Bruce, with some relief as the lights of the Presidential residence appeared over the ridge ahead. There were times when he found it difficult to reconcile the more feminine aspects of Helen Lindstrom's character with her coolly efficient Corps officer persona. It was largely his fear that one might eventually spill over into the other that had been responsible for his difficult decision several years previously. There were plenty of good bedmates around for a man with his looks and position, but only one second-in-command for *Venturer Twelve*.

"The trouble with this kind of wingding," said Admiral Junius Farragut Carter, making heavy weather of trying to juggle a plateful of *vol au vent* and salad, a fork, and a glass of champagne with only the statutory maximum of hands. "The trouble with this kind of wingding is that you either get a reasonable, sit-down knife and fork meal, during which you have the arse bored off you by a series of long-winded speeches, or, like this evening, you have to listen to the speeches first, then scrabble around in a mob, fighting to grab something from a pile of cold odds and ends."

"Sometimes I suspect that you're just not a social animal, Admiral," Helen Lindstrom said, eyeing the precarious balancing act. "Look, there's a free table over there. Why don't we grab it?"

"Sound tactics, Commander," said Carter, who even in his full dress World Admiral's uniform still managed to look squat as a bug and twice as homely. "Let's go. Goddammit!" This last as a portly, dinner-suited civilian passed close by, jogging Carter's elbow slightly and dislodging two lettuce leaves and a radish.

"There, that's more comfortable isn't it?" said Helen, as Carter shed his burdens and settled in the chair opposite her.

"Commander Lindstrom, I've said it before and I'll say it again—aside from being the best-looking piece of tail in the whole Corps, you are a first-class organizer."

"Why, Admiral!" grinned Helen, who was well used to Carter's colorful use of language. "You say the sweetest things. How come Velma let you off the leash tonight?"

"She's spending a couple of weeks with her sister over in England," said the Admiral. "You know, the one with the teeth, who has this thing about horses."

Helen sipped her champagne. "Frankly, I don't know how she dare leave a young dog like you on the loose for a whole fourteen days. How are things at Blue Mountain?"

Carter prodded suspiciously at the flaky pastry of his *vol au vent*. "We're moving along slowly."

"Yes? I heard you'd lost Koninburger."

"That opinionated Kraut!"

"Maybe so, but surely his equations are the best lead you've had so far?"

"Hmm. . .not bad, not bad at all," Carter said,

chewing at a forkful. "Say, these darned things are hot, did you know that? You figure there's any garlic in there? I get this pain right in the center of my chest. . ."

"Koninburger's equations," persisted Helen.

"It takes more than a pile of scribblings on paper to throw a ship into Warp Drive," grunted Carter. "We'll lick it—give us time and we'll lick it. . .provided Detweiler and his crowd of penny-pinchers don't clamp down on the appropriations."

"But surely the loss of Koninburger—?"

"Young woman, would you like to hear me really swear?" said Carter, the unruly greying fuzz on his round head bristling. "If so, just keep mentioning that name. Koninburger is out—O-U-T, out, and that suits me just fine." His voice raised in pitch as he assumed an atrociously exaggerated accent. " 'Please, Admiral, would you not be incoming to my laboratory when I am in the labor of contemplation. Your vibrations they are so disturbing. Mine dear Admiral, the possibility you are speaking of, it quite out of the question. My latent geo-nostalgic psychosis would simply not permit—' "

"Difficult, huh?"

"Bloody impossible!" growled Carter. "But that's the trouble when you start dealing with blasted civilians. No sense of priorities, and no discipline. I told the President myself only the other day—"

"But *he's* a civilian," Helen pointed out.

"Don't quibble, girl! In any case, technically speaking he is Commander-in-chief of the Corps, so how the hell can he be? Anyway, I said to him, 'Henry, I've got a team here that will lick the Warp Drive problem without Koninburger. But if you think you can pull this other deal, even if it doesn't work, I'll still be pleased to see—' " Carter stopped suddenly in mid-flow. "You know, I'm sure there's garlic in this."

"Have some more champagne," said Helen. "They say you'll live forever if you drink enough of it."

"Then by damn we'll both have some more," said Carter, lumbering to his feet. "No sense in fooling around with odd glasses—I'll get a bottle."

Helen watched with an expression of fond amusement on her face as he made his way through the chattering throng around the bar with all the subtlety of a bull elephant in full charge.

"Good to see you again, Tom." The tall blond man in the plain dark-blue uniform of a merchant space officer thrust out his hand.

Tom Bruce grinned his pleasure as he returned the firm grip. "I caught a glimpse of you way over the other side of the hall during the back-scratching session, but you seemed to disappear afterwards."

"We got stuck at Poppa's personal congratulation orgy up in the President's private lounge," said Robert Prince. "Elsa's still with him, but I managed to sneak down and see if there were any human beings around. I see your second-in-command has got herself lumbered with old Carter."

"Yes, that's quite a thing they have going there," Bruce said, glancing towards the table on the other side of the room where Helen and the Admiral were chatting animatedly.

"I thought at one time that you and she were going to make it," Prince said.

"We had our moments," Bruce said.

"It looked more like marriage."

"You know that would never work—two serving Corps officers."

"She could have opted out."

"I couldn't ask any woman, particularly Helen, to do that for me."

"The Corps takes everything, doesn't it?"

"If you don't want the obligations, you don't have to sign the form," Bruce said with a shrug. "They warn you."

"And what fourteen-year-old kid with his head full of stardust ever listened to any warnings?" said Prince. "Even if he wasn't blinded by the usual romanticized ideal of the CORPS, he would still have no idea of the kind of problems that can come up later on, as a man grows older. As for the women, sometimes I think it's even worse. You've seen them in a hundred Officers' Messes—flat-chested, leathery-faced creatures who either drink too much or go off in some weird sexual orbit."

Bruce nodded. "Yes, I've seen them. But who's to say that they'd be any happier changing diapers and working as a house robot for some slob of a man with half their brains?"

"There's more to a marriage than that," Prince said.

Bruce eyed his old friend with suspicion. "What are you doing—missionary work? I get my share of sex, and plenty of variety."

"And she?" Prince nodded in the direction of Helen Lindstrom.

"I don't see what that has to do with it."

"Yes, you do—and it hurts sometimes, doesn't it, when you know she's laying some slob just to relieve the ache of the old hormones? And with a body like that, don't try to tell me she *doesn't*."

"What are you trying to do, needle me?" Bruce said. "That's the way things are, and there's nothing to be done about it."

"There might be," Prince said.

"Now what's that supposed to mean?"

"I can think of a way that you could have your cake and eat it—Helen too," said Prince. "The post of Fleet Director at Excelsior pays a lot better than the Corps, and you'd need a good assistant."

"You're offering me a job?"

"I can't think of a more suitable candidate," Prince said.

"Now just a minute—*you're* Fleet Director of Excelsior, aren't you?"

"At the moment—but I expect to be moving up soon."

"Up?"

"Poppa Niebohr named me as his successor at the last board meeting. From now on I shall be working more closely with him."

"Like learning how to use money and power to crush anybody who stands in your way?"

"Now Tom, I'll admit that Poppa has cut a few corners in the past, but things are different now."

"Those Niebohrs really got through to you, didn't they? How can you be so simple-minded?"

"Because that's the way I love him," interrupted a deep, slightly husky female voice.

Both men turned to look at the stunning raven-haired beauty, whose deep-tanned body was framed rather than covered by a brilliant turquoise evening dress. Only in the bold hawklike nose was there any apparent resemblance to her father, and in her case the feature was an asset, lending a striking individuality to her entire face. Looking at Elsa Niebohr in the flesh for the first time was like seeing an original Leonardo sculpture after previously having experienced nothing but cheap reproductions. The contrasts between her and Helen Lindstrom were so great, in so many ways, that seen side by side it would have been difficult to believe they were females of the same species. And yet, as he stared down at the tiny woman, who was a whole head and shoulders shorter than himself, he found himself moved in such an undeniably sexual manner that a lance of pain seemed to pierce the pit of his stomach.

"Commander Bruce, I've been looking forward to meeting you for such a long time." The voice was a musical, throaty purr with a hint of laughter near the surface, and the dark eyes held his in a steady challenge as she held out one hand towards him.

"Mrs. Prince. . ." Bruce held the tiny, perfect fingers in his own large hand for a moment, aware that he was being bewitched and ashamed of his own susceptibility. It seemed to him that he had never met a woman in his whole life who so epitomized the mystery and challenge of her sex. Beside Elsa Niebohr the beauty of Helen Lindstrom was as that of a glacier to an erupting volcano.

"Elsa, please," she said, drawing her hand away at last. "Robert has spoken of you so often that I feel we are already old friends. Now that we have met, we must see more of each other. How long will you be on Earth?"

"About three weeks. My ship is undergoing a refit."

"That's wonderful! You must join us next weekend at our place in Hierro; the swimming there is terrific at this time of the year."

"Yes, why don't you do that, Tom?" said Prince. "We could relax for a few days and have a real bull session."

"Well, I'm not sure. . ."

"Don't make up your mind now," Prince said. "I'll give you a call tomorrow. Perhaps you'd like to bring Helen Lindstrom along as well. We could talk some more on the subject I mentioned earlier."

"All right, I'll check on my duty commitments first thing in the morning," Bruce said, still acutely aware of the challenge in Elsa's dark eyes.

"Where's your father?" asked Prince, glancing round the crowded room.

"He stayed upstairs with the President," Elsa said. "I expect they'll be down in a while to do some token mingling. In the meantime, there's a wonderful band playing out there on the terrace. Why don't we dance?"

Prince shrugged, smiling at Bruce. "Duty calls, Tom. See you later."

Bruce watched as the tall blond man took hold of Elsa's arm and the two of them walked toward the open doorway. As he contemplated the way the woman's rounded yet slim buttocks moved, he became aware with even greater intensity of a lusting animal inside him that was joyfully contemplating the possibility of cuckolding his good friend. With a snort of self-disgust he turned away abruptly and headed toward the nearest bar.

Chapter Six

Once again we are being asked to sign an open check to subsidize this line of research— to authorize the spending of billions of credits on a project which has in three years yielded no positive results whatever. I realize that it is considered bad form in some quarters to criticize any activity that involves the Space Corps, but in our present economic situation can we afford to go on pouring money into this search for a Space Warp Drive?
Senator Charles Detweiler (addressing the Space Corps Appropriations Committee.)

Henry Fong, President of United Earth, stood on a balcony looking down onto the illuminated ornamental gardens of his residence. The sound of sweetly sentimental music floated through the warm air, carrying with it snatches of conversation and laughter. A small neat man, wearing a simple high-necked semi-uniform, he turned to his companion and smiled. "A great occasion, Elkan. You must feel very proud."

Elkan Niebohr's deep-set eyes looked down into the

52

smooth, slimmed-down Buddha face of one of the few living men for whose ability he had any real respect.

"I do indeed, Mr. President," he said in his careful, accented English. "But you didn't keep me up here just to listen to a repeat of my acceptance speech, did you? Why don't we just get down to cases?"

A flicker of pain passed over Fong's face in response to the insensitive occidental bluntness of his guest. There were times when he wondered just how such a man could ever have reached his present position as head of Earth's most influential and successful Colonization Corporation. Wondered—until he reminded himself that the great hulk of a body housed a ruthless ambition and a questing, ferocious intelligence, which even now, in the shadow of approaching old age, retained its dangerous potential. Elkan Niebohr was a man to be handled with care.

"It is a small matter," he said quietly. "But one that I thought would be best discussed privately between us. I believe that you have recently negotiated an understanding with Koninburger. May I inquire as to the nature of the arrangement?"

Niebohr's hawk-face was immediately alert, the hooded eyes watchful. "Mr. President, I don't think—"

"Very well, Elkan, if you so insist, I must tell *you*," said Fong, his tone still mild. "You have offered Koninburger the backing of your corporation's considerable resources in order to establish his own research and development program into a Warp Drive. The details of the conditions are unimportant, but I would guess that they entail the retention of a considerable percentage of interest in the proceeds of any such drive, should it be developed."

"I think it was one of your predecessors who stated that there is no crime in making a profit," said Niebohr.

"Provided that such a profit is not made at the expense of the human race."

The sandstone color of Niebohr's features darkened slightly. "Mr. President, you have no right to make such implications. In fact, coming as they do after your public speech of less than an hour ago, I must confess—"

"You misunderstand me," Fong cut in with quiet firmness. "I can do nothing but applaud your enterprise in offering your support to this project, with all the obligations it may entail. A lesser man would never have been so far-sighted. I'm certain that your board as a whole would have hesitated to accept such a commitment had you not presented them with the *fait accompli.*"

"Let's not kid each other, Mr. President," Niebohr said. "You know as well as I do what went on at that meeting. Gould and some of those other young rebels would have had my balls off if I hadn't played the deal close to my chest."

"And now Mr. Gould is no longer with us," Fong said pensively. "A sad loss."

Niebohr nodded. "An unfortunate accident. My lawyers are working in the interests of the bereaved widow and children now."

"So I understand," Fong said. "And Mr. Falangetti?"

"A cerebral hemorrhage," Niebohr said. "The paralysis is receding slightly, and the specialists say he may be able to talk again eventually. He's having the best treatment Excelsior can provide—my own personal physician is supervising."

"But it is unlikely he will be taking any active interest in the proceedings of your board for some time to come."

"Unfortunately, no."

"The almost simultaneous loss of two so talented young executives must have been a severe blow to you."

"A tragedy," said Niebohr, warily.

The two of them stood silent in the velvet darkness for several moments. The band on the terrace finished playing the sentimental ballad and launched abruptly into a screeching, fast-tempoed *Chav.* Henry Fong winced as a squealing electro-flute pierced at his ears.

"Shall we go inside?" he said, moving towards the glass doors of the balcony.

Reestablished in the privacy and comparative peace of the lounge, with the balcony doors closed behind them, Fong moved towards the bar.

"A drink, Elkan?"

Niebohr settled for a scotch with ice and soda, and Fong, who never drank alcohol, had a glass of plain soda. The two men sat down opposite each other in deep gold velour-covered armchairs.

"To return to your theme of profit," Fong said at length. "You realize that it may be some considerable time—if ever—before Koninburger is able to produce a workable drive with commercial applications?"

"Yes," Niebohr said. "But Koninburger is already consulting with the head of my engineering department about the construction of a test prototype."

"Ah yes, the prototype," Fong said. "Koninburger has, of course, told you that it was the discussions about just such a prototype that resulted in his final disagreement with Admiral Carter and his withdrawal from the Blue Mountain Project?"

Niebohr shrugged massively. "He didn't go into

detail. As far as I understand it, he and Carter didn't get along from the very beginning. I find that hardly surprising, considering Carter's record."

"A very distinguished Corps officer, but not one noted for his tact," said Fong. "He is, however, a great deal more foresighted and cautious than would appear from his boorish manner."

"Cautious?"

Fong nodded. "Men of Koninburger's type, on the other hand, tend to follow their own vision without sufficient regard for the possible consequences."

"You can't force him to go back to Blue Mountain," Niebohr said.

"My dear Elkan, I have not the slightest intention of trying," said Fong. "His unwilling cooperation would be completely useless to us."

"Then what are you talking about?" demanded Niebohr.

Fong permitted himself a small inward sigh. The man had absolutely no appreciation of the principle of obliquity. "Both you and I are laymen in this matter, and as such we must accept the judgment of our experts. Mine inform me that the testing of a prototype such as Koninburger has suggested could entail considerable danger. No one knows for certain, of course, but I am told that, in the event of such a mechanism functioning even briefly, there is at least a forty percent probability of its shifting itself and give-or-take a few hundred, say, a thousand cubic kilometers of its surroundings into what we will call for convenience a sub-spatial dimension."

Niebohr stared at the President. "I can't believe that! The way I understand it, this thing would be hardly more than a test-bench scale model."

"We are dealing here with forces of which we have no past experience. Carter assures me that this assessment is a valid one. Determined as he is to produce such a drive, he felt it his duty to inform me fully of the likely effects of such a sub-spatial shift—whether permanent or temporary—on the planet as a whole. At the very least, we could expect seismic activity of catastrophic proportions, with violent earthquakes, volcanic activity, and *tsunami*—at worst, there is a distinct possibility that Earth could be kicked out of orbit completely, either sunwards or out towards the trans-Plutonian darkness. The risk is far too great."

"Does Koninburger know of this?" asked Niebohr.

"Naturally he was kept fully informed at all stages," said Fong. "But he refuses to accept the figures. He insists that the field generated by the prototype drive could not possibly affect such an area—although he does admit that there is likely to be some local damage."

"Local?"

Fong shrugged. "An inexact term, but the one he used, nevertheless. I must confess, it seems to me that Koninburger is the kind of man who would go ahead and create this thing whatever the risk involved. I, on the other hand, must be more cautious."

"Does that mean that you've decided to abandon the Blue Mountain Project?"

"Our need of a Space Warp drive is acute. As you know, without it we haven't the slightest chance of defending ourselves against any Kilroy attack," said Fong. "On the other hand, it is clear that such dangerous experimentation cannot be carried on here on Earth. Admiral Carter and his team at Blue Mountain are all as fully aware of the risks involved as it is possible to be at this stage, and they have agreed to be transferred to a new base of operations on the unassigned planet known as Tarasco IV."

"That ball of barren mud!"

"Precisely," said Fong. "In the event of the gloomier predictions about the testing of the prototype being filled, such a ball of mud would be expendable."

"But why didn't Koninburger tell me any of this?" said Niebohr. He managed to conceal his unease; he had hoped that his grand gesture to Koninburger would appear good.

"Possibly because, as I said earlier, he disagrees with Carter's figures," said Fong. "He would in any case be unlikely to draw your attention to such unfavorable possibilities when soliciting your financial backing for his project. I trust you have not committed yourself too deeply?"

Niebohr's dark eyebrows bunched dangerously above his deep-set eyes. "I've given him what amounts to an unlimited open credit, so long as he can rationalize the expenditure as legitimate research expenses."

Fong sipped his soda, nodding. "I see. Well, I don't see how you can be too much out of pocket on the deal, because the only research he is going to be able to do will have to be on a theoretical level. Obviously, in view of the risks involved, we can't allow him to build a prototype drive here on Earth. What he does elsewhere is, of course, another matter."

"Elsewhere?"

"I was thinking in terms of one of the undeveloped planets in your sector," said Fong. "There are three in the Kepler system alone. You could establish an experimental station on one of them, just as we are doing on Tarasco IV."

"Good God, man! Have you any idea of what that would cost?" exploded Niebohr.

"I have indeed," said Fong with a rueful smile. "Right down to the last credit, if you really want to know. Senator Detweiler has been fighting us all the way on the appropriations for the project."

"But you're going ahead?"

"My dear Elkan, if our race is to survive, there is no alternative," said Fong. "We have had our warnings on Minos and Kepler planets—the next time the aliens may strike at the home system. The Warp Drive is essential for our survival. That is why I urge you to go ahead with your own project, whatever the cost."

Niebohr contemplated his almost empty glass, his heavy face grim. "It's all very well for you to talk that way, Mr. President," he said at length. "But the kind of project you're talking about is the business of the government, not a commercial firm like Excelsior. I have to answer to my board and stockholders, and they have little taste for philanthropy, especially at their expense."

"Oh come now, Elkan," chided Fong. "Don't try to tell me that you can't handle that kind of opposition. Your excellent young son-in-law, Commander Prince, has already familiarized them with some of the essential arguments. I'm sure you're capable of making them understand that in the long run the integrity of our solar system is their finest investment. Anything less would place them in the position of a man who refuses to spend a few credits on candles, then breaks his neck on the stairway during a power failure."

"I'll have to think it over," Niebohr said guardedly. "As you say, there wouldn't be too much difficulty involved in finding a suitable planet, but at the moment every ship in our fleet is running to a tight schedule. Apart from that, there would be the job of recruiting suitable people to work on the project."

"I don't think you'd have a great deal of difficulty there," said Fong. "There must be a large number who would be only too eager for the opportunity of being associated with Koninburger. . ." He paused for a moment, drawing the tip of his right finger around the rim of his empty glass, sensing its rounded smoothness. "As I see it, your main obstacle is going to be Koninburger himself," he added musingly.

"Koninburger?" repeated Niebohr, glaring at his host in perplexity.

"Obviously he hasn't told you the nature of his final disagreement with Carter," Fong said. "Things had been pretty stormy between them all along the line, but they managed until Carter quite rightly came to the decision that prototype testing would have to take place somewhere like Tarasco IV. Apart from refusing to believe Carter's figures, Koninburger stated quite categorically that he would not under any circumstances leave Earth."

"But that's ridiculous!" Niebohr said. "Why would he make such a statement?"

"For what—to him at least—appears to be a very good reason," said Fong. "It seems that this eminent and progressive scientist has only been off Earth once in his life, when at the age of five years he accompanied his parents on a round trip to the Moon. Koninburger's father was an endocrinologist, and he was addressing a convention at the Geriatric Center about some work he had been doing on pituitary regulation with relation to aging. Or at least that was the intention. In the event, he never got to read his paper, because the young Hans Koninburger came down with a distressing and potentially lethal combination of symptoms that made it imperative for him to be shipped back to Earth if he was to survive."

"Now just a minute," Niebohr said. "Are you trying to tell me that with all the medical talent and resources on Moon they were incapable of treating a sick child?"

"There is only one treatment for such an illness," Fong said. "Our present Corps Surgeon General, Admiral Hurwitz, made the diagnosis and ordered that the boy be flown back to Earth immediately in a scout ship. Two minutes after landing all symptoms had completely disappeared, and the young Koninburger was happily guzzling a chocolate malt in the Officers' Mess."

"Geo-Nostalgic Psychosis?" said Niebohr.

"Koninburger would have died if he hadn't been returned to Earth within twenty-four hours. Hurwitz knew that from his Corps experience," said Fong. "Most cases are fortunately less acute, but even so, the condition accounts for almost twenty-five percent of medical discharges from the Corps. But you must be familiar with those facts. It happens among colonists as well."

Niebohr nodded. "Solar had an epidemic a couple of years ago, out on Deneb. They shipped over two hundred people back to Earth, and a third of them didn't make it. We've been lucky—just the odd case here and there, and usually in the less acute form."

"Under the circumstances you can understand why Koninburger was less than willing to take part in the Tarasco IV operation," said Fong. "Even though his one and only direct experience of the disease was over forty years ago, he was unwilling even to submit to tests aimed at discovering whether there had been any remission."

"You mean he may have grown out of it?"

"Such cases have been known," said Fong. "At least, it would have been worthwhile to try and find out."

Niebohr leaned his bulky body forward in the chair and stared intently into the egg-smooth face of Fong. "Mr. President, why are you telling me all this?" he asked.

Fong smiled blandly. "My dear Elkan, in order to make sure that you do not find yourself saddled with the responsibility for the death of one of our most eminent scientists—why else?"

"You're sure there's no other reason?"

The President's smile broadened. "Let me put it this way. As far as relationships between Koninburger and Carter—or any other Corps officer, for that matter— are concerned, the situation has gone too far for retrieval. Obviously he has a valuable contribution to make to the development of a Warp Drive, but he is completely incapable of cooperating with our people. If, on the other hand, he were running his own establishment, with a completely free hand—"

"But you yourself have just explained precisely why he can't do that," said Niebohr. "A prototype cannot be built here on Earth if your figures are correct— and I for one don't intend to rely on the chance that they *aren't*—and Koninburger cannot leave Earth because of his latent Geo-Nostalgic Psychosis."

"Elkan, my presentation speech this evening may have contained a number of rather fulsome compliments, as is the custom on such occasions, but it was in the main a sincere tribute to your ingenuity and persistence, for which I have a great deal of respect. This being so, I have not the slightest doubt that you will eventually think of a way to overcome this small obstacle. Indeed, you will deserve all the praise grateful humanity can shower upon you, if you succeed where world government fails." The President rose to his feet. "But I have monopolized your attention quite long enough. Everyone will be wondering what has happened to the guest of honor. Shall we go down?"

Chapter Seven

A woman is more responsive to a man's for-getfulness than to his attentions.

JANIN

The first glow of dawn was beginning to show in the East as Tom Bruce veered out of his traffic lane and headed the flycar in toward Corps Base Mel-pond. He was feeling more than a little depressed and aware that he had drunk rather too much whiskey. He had never been particularly fond of socializing, and this evening had ended up by being even more boring than most. He had started off in reasonably good spirits, feeling comfortably superior to the chattering, useless crowd of party-goers, but after several drinks his thoughts had begun to turn inward in a kind of self-examination that was unusual for him.

Alone in the bustling, glittering throng, he had begun to wonder if his own life was after all quite as meaningful or worthwhile as he had always assumed. Bob Prince's remark about the drying, shriveling effect of Corps life on women had probably been the initial stimulus that had started him on the track, but he had found himself speculating if some similar kind of process might take place in men as well. Devotion to duty carried certain satisfactions, but there were times when a man needed something more—some more personal reassurance of his humanity, perhaps.

He had little doubt that meeting Prince again was responsible for this trend of thought. The man's confidence and obvious happiness had forced Bruce to revise his original opinion that Prince had somehow sold out by resigning his commission and moving over to the commercial sector. If Prince *had* sold out, he had evidently made a good deal, finding a warmth and stability that the Corps could never provide, despite all the brave talk about *esprit de corps*. And Elsa. . . The memory of those dark, intense features and that sleekly desirable body kindled a surge of envy. There was a woman who knew how to keep a man happy —even if she was making a fool of him at the same time.

He frowned as he made a clumsy landing and began to trundle the car towards his parking space. Would he settle for what Bob Prince had, or something like it? If so, the opportunity was there: a good, well-paid job, with a comfortable home here on Earth, instead of wasting months on end patroling the infinities of space—months during which he, as captain, was always on parade, compelled by the needs of discipline to live in an atmosphere of godlike aloofness. He had only to say the word to Prince and the door would be opened to a new, affluent life, a life in which he would no longer be a symbol of authority but a normal human being.

A hint of the old guilt began to creep back as he got out of the flycar, but he slammed the door angrily, thrusting it from him. He had given nearly twenty years of his life to the Corps. Surely that was enough. No one could say that he had not fulfilled his obligations. Now? A fresh beginning—a new, more meaningful existence, with time for human feeling and emotion. . .time to enjoy himself. . .

Alone? The question formed itself as he walked across the concrete toward the entrance of the Officers' Quarters, and the answer flashed into his mind with an immediacy that was a clear implication of its truth. What was it Prince had said? *'You could have your cake and eat it—Helen too.'*

Yes. . .that was what he wanted. But if the step was to be taken they had to take it together, the two of them—then it would have some real meaning. Filled with the immediacy and truth of his new decision, he quickened his pace. This was something that had to be talked about and settled now. There could be no sense in waiting until tomorrow, when they would both be immersed again in rigid, official routine.

He paused for a moment outside the door of her quarters before knocking. He had seen her leave the reception somewhere around one A.M. escorted by Junius Carter. What if she was not alone? Not with Carter—the old man was too devoted to his Velma to get involved in that kind of thing—but with someone else. . . Some other Corps officer who needed to—what was Prince's phrase?—*relieve the ache of the old hormones.*

He knocked abruptly. The sound, much louder than he had intended, rattled enormously along the bare, aseptic corridor.

"Tom! Kind of late for calling, isn't it?" She stood in the half-open doorway, honey-blonde hair hanging loose to her shoulders, statuesque body draped in a pale-blue, semi-transparent wrapper.

"Did I wake you?"

"Well no—as a matter of fact I was reading. I had a shower when I got home and it seemed to wake me up." She stood to one side as he entered the room and closed the door behind him.

The bare, official room was relieved by subtle hints of her femininity, and the familiar spicy tang of her body perfume caught at his throat, kindling such a flood of tenderness that for a moment he could do nothing but stand and look at her in silence.

"Tom—what is the matter with you?" She moved a couple of steps towards him, then stopped. "God! You smell as if you'd been marinated in ten-year-old scotch for a week. Are you drunk?"

"A little. . ." he admitted. "Maybe just enough."

"Enough for what?" Her deep-blue eyes were wary now.

"To give me the courage to admit that I may have been wrong about certain things," he said, "You and me, for instance. We both know that neither of us is any good to anyone else, however much we—"

"So that's it!" Her voice cut in on him, stopping him dead, and he stared open-mouthed into her suddenly hardened, ice-queen features. "You slob! You drunken bum!"

He recoiled before her fury, mumbling, confused, and suddenly aware that he really *was* drunk.

"You picked the wrong place and the wrong time, Tom." Her voice was flat and crushingly scornful. "If you want to find somebody to ride the hard-on you've been nursing ever since you clapped eyes on that goddammed parakeet Elsa Niebohr, you'd better go along to that twenty-credit cathouse down the road from the enlisted men's quarters. Now get out!"

She flung the door of the room open again and he left without a word. Her speech had said it all, making him realize fully for the first time just what he had done to her that night when, so smug in his conceptions of duty and discipline, he had told her that their relationship must end. The words didn't matter; they were just the outward manifestation—lost, ephemeral sounds. What did matter was the hardening scar tissue deep in her mind that must have been eating into and drying her womanhood ever since that night, so that now it was too late—too late for both of them. She would never fully trust herself to another man—and he. . .he would never forgive himself for what he had done to her in the sacred name of the Corps.

"Bugger the Corps!" he snarled, slamming the door of his quarters behind him. He walked unsteadily across to the cocktail cabinet and began to peel the foil from the stopper of a fresh bottle of Ballantine's. . . .

Chapter Eight

*If the rich could hire other people to die for
them, the poor would make a wonderful living.*
                                    YIDDISH PROVERB

Doctor Anderson Fane was dark and catlike. He
sat in the chair behind his large dark oak desk in
a manner so utterly relaxed that several times Niebohr had the disturbing impression that he was actually asleep. This impression did nothing to improve
his temper. He was accustomed to having people pay
attention when he talked, and when he paid them
the kind of money Fane demanded for a consultation,
he felt entitled to at least a display of interest. Finish-
ing his carefully prepared explanation, Niebohr found
himself grasping the arms of his chair and glaring at
the near-somnolent psychiatrist. As the silence in the
immaculately insulated consulting room lengthened,
his rage began to grow like steam pressure mounting
inside a grossly overheated boiler. Any moment now
it would demand the release of telling this handsome, expensively dressed charlatan a few home
truths about his behavior.

69

The imminent explosion was averted as Fane's eyes opened wider. Here again, they were in keeping with the catlike image, being of a strangely luminous greeny-gold. The smile, displaying a set of very white teeth that held a suggestion of carnivorous sharpness, was evidently more in the nature of a formal preliminary to speech than any expression of humor.

"What you're really asking me, Mr. Niebohr, is whether there is any extrasensory perception element involved in Geo-Nostalgia."

"I wasn't aware of asking any such question," growled Niebohr. "All I want to know is if it would be feasible, by the careful control of his environment down to the smallest detail, so much so that he would have to accept the evidence of all his normal senses that he was on Earth, to prevent such a patient from having an attack of the disease."

"Precisely." Fane stroked the air with one languid, long-fingered hand. "The evidence of all his *normal* senses. Speaking of a hypothetical case, I'm afraid it is impossible to be categorical. When you speak of normal senses I take it that you are speaking of sight, hearing, touch, smell and taste."

"Naturally."

Fane moved his head from side to side in a gesture of maddening superiority which conveyed his tolerant pity for the limitations of the lay mind. "My dear Mr. Niebohr, if this conversation were to have taken place, say, fifty years ago, I would probably have been able to give you a categorical answer. Unless I was possessed of certain extremely *avant garde* ideas, I would surely have said to you that, provided the environment were meticulously controlled in the manner you suggest, the patient would be unlikely to succumb to the disease. However, the work of Friedhofer and Blount has opened up new areas of uncertainty so vast that today he would be a fool who presumed to make generalizations about the limits or the functions of the human mind. Not to bore you with too much detail, let me merely point out that according to Blount there is experimental evidence to indicate the existence of at least four senses other than those which are traditionally regarded as normal in human beings. It is very rarely that all of these are found in the same person, but should even one of them be present in the case you are speaking of, the results could be disastrous."

"Supposing the person concerned were in fact to be limited to the old-fashioned five senses," said Niebohr.

Fane shrugged. "In that case it would be an interesting experiment—if a dangerous one. The slightest hint of strangeness—a word, a gesture on the part of any person in contact with the patient—might set off a train of reaction and bring on an attack."

"But there would be a chance of success?"

"That depends on a large number of factors," Fane said. "Not the least of which would be the period of time involved. The entire thing would be on a constant knife-edge, and such an equilibrium cannot be maintained indefinitely. The operation would have to be supervised and planned down to the smallest detail—constant surveillance and feedback techniques would have to be developed. . ."

Neibohr felt a flush of triumph that did something to restore both his temper and his battered ego, as he realized that he had the psychiatrist really interested at last. It was always the same with these experts—feed their vanity and let them walk over you for a while, and they fell into your lap like ripe plums.

". . .all the other people in the environment. Possibly some kind of hypnotic technique might be used in their preparation. Budweiser mentions in his paper on the training of—"

"Doctor Fane," interrupted Niebohr. "Would you be prepared to accept the post of consultant on such a project? A year's contract, initially, with an option on either side of renewal for a further period of six months."

Fane's smooth forehead creased in an uncharacteristic frown. "Mr. Niebohr, I have my practice to think of—my patients depend on me. . ."

Neibohr was in an area he understood now. In the matter of buying and selling people *he* was the expert. He glanced around the well-equipped consulting room appraisingly. "What do you make in a year, Fane? A hundred thousand—maybe a hundred and fifty? I'll pay you a million, guaranteed, whether the project is successful or not. With that kind of money you can afford to pay a locum."

Fane was sitting forward in his chair now, the languor entirely gone from his posture. "I'm not sure that the undertaking is ethical. There would be considerable danger to the patient—"

Neibohr rose to his feet, towering over the man behind the desk. "And a million bonus on successful completion," he said. "Think about it, and call me before six o'clock this evening." He turned abruptly and walked out of the consulting room, his face a mask and his mind filled with the satisfaction of another deal. Nothing would stop him.

Tom Bruce opened gummy eyelids to find himself staring up into a familiar, grinning face.

" 'Morning, Captain," said C.P.O. Dockridge, holding out a bubbling glass of clear liquid. "Try this."

Painfully aware of the thundering inside his head, Bruce raised himself on one elbow and downed the glass of seltzer. The liquid met head on with the juices of his roiling stomach and exploded in a resounding burp.

"Boy, you must really have tied one on last night," said Dockridge, shaking his head in sympathy. "I got the picture when I saw the bottle and the way your things were strewn around, so I thought I'd leave you lie awhile."

"Lie? What time is it?" Bruce jerked upright. The sudden movement did nothing to improve the condition of his head.

"Half after eleven," said Dockridge.

"Hell!" barked Bruce. "I had a meeting of officers scheduled for ten A.M. You knew that; why didn't you wake me?"

"Not to worry, Captain. Commander Lindstrom said she'd handle it. She was around at the crack of dawn, all bright-eyed and bushy-tailed, and she's been down at the yard since seven-thirty chasing the hell out of everybody." Dockridge grinned confidentially. "If you ask my opinion, this earthbound life doesn't suit any of us. The sooner we get out into space and into the old routine, the better."

"Nobody asked your goddammed opinion, Doc!" snapped Bruce, swinging his legs over the edge of the bed and realizing for the first time that he was still wearing his vest and shorts. "And this morning I can really live without your two-bit philosophizing, understood?"

"Yes *sir*," said Dockridge, still hovering. "Can I get you some breakfast, maybe?"

"Out!" barked Bruce.

Doc shrugged his shoulders and left, his prosthetic leg dragging slightly.

Some twenty minutes later, shaved and showered, Bruce returned to the bedroom feeling slightly more human and began to dress. He was just zipping the front of his jacket when he heard the vid in the lounge chime. He walked through and punched the ON button.

"Hallo there!" said the smiling image of Robert Prince.

" 'Morning," said Bruce.

"You're looking a bit finely drawn," Prince said.

"So my batman just informed me," Bruce said. "I'll live."

"Glad to hear that. I called about next weekend. Will you be able to make it?"

"Well, sure, I'd like to very much."

"And the lady?"

"Huh?"

"Helen Lindstrom—you'll be bringing her along?"

"I. . .I think not."

"Pity. . ." Prince said. "But there'll be a couple of other interesting females along, so you should find it interesting. You know Veronica Marsden?"

"Know is hardly the word—I've seen her several hundred times on TV, of course."

"You'll like her; she's fun—with a capital F, if you follow me?"

"I thought you and Elsa—?"

"Why sure we are—I'm only telling you what they say," said Prince, laughing. "But *you're* unattached."

Unattached. . . That was for sure, thought Bruce

grimly. Whatever had once existed between himself and Helen could never happen again.

"We leave from Clarke Field at midnight on Friday —all right?" said Prince.

"Yes, sure, fine. . . Thanks, Bob. I'll look forward to it."

"Me too—we've got a lot to talk over. 'Bye."

"'Bye." Bruce switched off and turned away from the screen. A lot to talk over. . . Yes, a whole new future. There was no going back careerwise, any more than there was in his love life. The Corps had ruined what existed between him and Helen Lindstrom— he had little doubt of that—grinding it down and fitting it into pigeon holes of duty and obedience. Prince had been right—the Corps took everything. . .

But not anymore. This weekend would be the beginning of a new phase in the career of Tom Bruce. Animated by a new resolution, he went out.

Chapter Nine

It is very unusual for salmon native to the waters of Earth to migrate during their first year of existence, when they are in the stage of development known as parr. The characteristic marks of a parr are ten or eleven dark bands on an orange ground along the middle of each side of the fish and round black spots on the gill covers. During this period the fish remains in the fresh water where it was hatched, returning to the sea when it moves into the smolt stage, during which the dark bands gradually disappear and the orange is replaced by silver. Soon after this the characteristic silvery appearance of the adult salmon is attained.

In salmon native to Orphelin—or, to express their origin more correctly, salmon which are descendants of the fry introduced into the fresh-water pools and rivers of the southern islands of the Orphelin ocean some twenty-five years previously—the process of maturation through the stages of parr and smolt has been so telescoped that the fish is manifestly adult at the age of six months and begins the process of migration back to the breeding grounds, which have been established in those same pools and rivers, shortly afterwards.

The spawning process is acknowledged to be a particularly exhausting one, and very few male fish survive to breed a second time amongst those native to Earth. The spent fish —known as "kelts" or "slats"—are in a very enfeebled condition, and on the long and arduous return journey to the sea many succumb to disease, injuries or starvation, or fall easy prey to their enemies. On Orphelin, however, this journey proves much less hazardous. There are a far lesser number of predators and very few parasites, such as the gill-infesting Salmincola, and the bacillus Salmonispestis is practically unknown. Thus, my observations indicate that some 90% of the kelts survive the return journey to the sea, where abundant food soon restores them to their normal condition.

This recovery is so swift and complete that it is not uncommon to find a fish making its way once more in the migration to the breeding grounds less than three months after its return to the sea. Thus, whereas an Earth salmon will spawn at the most three times during its life, on Orphelin a fish may do so anywhere up to ten times. This fact, combined with the above-mentioned lack of predators and disease, goes a long way towards explaining the extraordinary population explosion that has taken place amongst the Orphelin salmon.

It is my contention that during the decade and a half that has elapsed since its introduction to the waters of Orphelin, Salar Salar has undergone some kind of evolutionary process —mutation would perhaps be a more correct term—which has resulted in a greatly accel-

*erated life cycle and an enormous increase in
fecundity. This being so, I feel that there may
be some justification for a suggestion that the
fish produced by this phenomenon should be
regarded as a new sub-species, for which the
most appropriate name would be Salar Salar
Orphelis.*

> Extract from Chapter Three of *The
> Anadromous Fishes of Orphelin III*
> by Angus Alexander MacGuinness,
> M.Sc., B.Sc., M.B. (Edinburgh,
> published by Ratcliffe & Toomey.)

When MacGuinness returned from his inspection of
the tanks Bill Emery was still outside the hut tidying
up the area between it and the flycar. MacGuinness
watched the man at work for a few minutes, at the
same time skillfully lighting himself a cigar. From inside the hut he could hear the sounds of Alan Emery
preparing their evening meal. Apart from a certain
facility for making porridge, MacGuinness's mastery of
the culinary art was limited to the single, although
admittedly regal, masterpiece of Saumon MacGuinness. In any case, there were a great many other
tasks pressing on his attention, tasks for which he
alone of the three had the training and knowledge.
Over the past few months he had developed a considerable attachment for the two Emerys. Hard-working and uncomplaining men—he could not have
asked for a more congenial pair of companions on an
expedition of this nature.

"Och! I think you can safely give it a rest now,
Bill, and take a look at the sunset," he said at length,
waving his hand toward the majestic redness of the

western horizon. "Yon clouds are a work of art, no less."

"God's work," said Bill Emery, a curious, quiet smile on his weatherbeaten face as he looked towards the horizon.

"Aye. That's true enough. And He certainly did you people here on Orphelin Three proud. It's a marvel you haven't all changed into idle lotus-eaters."

"Idle hands, Professor?" Bill shook his greying, tight-curled head. "That's not our way—nor His."

"I'll not argue with that," said MacGuinness. A natural agnostic himself, he had learned to respect the quiet faith of these colonists as a necessary part of their existence. Orphelin Three might be a near-paradise, but the very thought of the vast distance that separated this planet from Earth and the solar system carried with it a constant threat. In purely practical terms, the idea that the same Creator watched over Orphelin was helpful. Leaving Bill to his work, he walked on past and into the hut.

Alan Emery was standing by the stove, a blue-and-white-striped butcher's apron tied around his stocky middle. Even without the sight of the half-empty glass in his left hand and the bottle that stood on the table, the source of the glow on the colonist's rugged features would have been obvious. Alan's susceptibility to the charms of Bell's Scotch was beginning to be an anxiety to MacGuinness. The last thing he wanted to do was to offend Alan, but sooner or later he knew he was going to have to point out that a man needed a special kind of head to drink the stuff in such quantities without ill-effects.

"Land crab salad, followed by steak and onions, with tomatoes and french-fries on the side, and pineapple slices with cream to finish. How does that grab you, Professor?" Alan said.

"Like a vice," MacGuinness said approvingly. "Back on Earth I see *real* meat maybe once a week, and even then it's usually like bootleather." He took a glass and poured himself a generous measure from the fast-dwindling bottle. "Take my advice, Alan—don't you ever go home. You people here have got it made."

"This is my home, Professor," Alan said, grinning. He finished his drink at a gulp and reached for the bottle.

"By adoption, sure," MacGuinness said. "And that's the best way to think of it. Nobody with any sense would want to go back after over twenty years of this kind of life. . . The last few months has unsettled me, I can tell you."

"No, Professor, you misunderstand," Alan said. "Orphelin is the only planet I ever knew. *I was born here.*"

"Aye, and you can pull the other one. It's got bells on," MacGuinness said, laughing. "Och! You'll be claiming next to be an autochthon sprung from the very soil of Orphelin, and that you and Bill were there to meet the colonization ship when it landed twenty-five years ago. No—that's carrying the idea of adoption too far."

"I'm not joking, Professor," Alan said. "Bill was on the ship, naturally, because he's one of the original settlers."

MacGuinness's laughter faded in the face of the stocky man's quiet solemnity. "And *you?*"

Alan shrugged. "I was just—how's the saying?—a gleam in his eye at the time, not due to make my appearance on the scene for something like twenty-seven months after that."

MacGuinness felt something move deep in the pit of his stomach as he looked into the weatherbeaten face of the apparently middle-aged man. "How old are you, Alan?" He asked the question fearfully, because his acute mind had already moved on ahead, suggesting the answer.

"Pushing twenty-three," said Alan cheerfully.

"Are you married?"

"Why sure—twelve years ago next Landing Anniversary," Alan said. "Matter of fact, the old lady and I are expecting to be grandparents any time now. By the time we get back. . . Say, Professor, there something wrong?" This last as MacGuinness turned abruptly and headed out of the hut, almost colliding in the doorway with Bill Emery, who was on the way in.

"Going out, Professor?" Bill said.

"Something I forgot," mumbled MacGuinness, preoccupied with his own racing thoughts. "Is the flycar door unlocked?"

"Why sure, Professor," Bill said. "But you're not going to take her up now, are you? I thought dinner was nearly ready."

"I'll no' be long," MacGuinness said. "I just remembered something I left out of that report I radioed into Josiahtown. If I call right now I might catch it before they've relayed it back to Earth."

He hurried across toward the flycar. The sky had deepened into purple twilight now, and the moon had not yet risen. There was no wind, and the whole island seemed unnaturally still, the only sound the sighing of small wavelets as they broke on the stones of the beach. To the ears of Angus MacGuinness they sounded like the measured breathing of some gigantic, satisfied animal—the planet that he himself had called a near-paradise only a few minutes before. He shuddered, cursing himself for not having interpreted, before this, the import of the thousands of pieces of evidence that had been staring him in the face ever since the day he landed—small things, true, but ones that now fitted with shattering clarity into the overall picture. True, he had been sent to Orphelin to report on fish, not human beings—but that was no excuse for such blindness.

As he opened up the door of the flycar he heard Alan Emery's voice from the direction of the hut. "Don't be too long, Professor. This steak isn't going to keep rare forever."

Alan, who was twenty-two years old and looked in his late forties—older than Bill, his own father. Alan, who would surely be senile before he reached the age of thirty.

MacGuinness asked himself why these people accepted such a situation. It must have been obvious, to the original colonizers at least, that something was terribly wrong. The answer, when it came, was all too obvious. What was their alternative? People like the Orphelin colonists, with their pioneering spirit of independence, would rather make any sacrifice than be dispossessed of the world that had become their home and be returned to the confines of overcrowded Earth. Their investment of blood, toil and sweat in a future on Orphelin Three was a commitment that they could not abandon without a struggle. And he had no doubt that such a struggle had been going on quietly for years now, beneath the cover of a planetwide conspiracy of silence—a desperate search for the cause of the shortened life-span trend, and when that was isolated, for a cure.

Visitors from Earth were infrequent on Orphelin,

most of them freighter crews enjoying a short leave between arrival and reloading. Such men were in search of a good time, and they would hardly be likely to look with a scientist's critical eye on the society of the planet. Even he himself had not begun to suspect the existence of the secret until now. Perhaps he never would have if it had not been for Alan Emery's alcohol-induced indiscretion.

Now he realized that he was faced with a whole planetary population in a state of mind similar to that of a person who, suffering from some loathsome, socially unacceptable disease, attempts to treat himself, resorting to quack remedies and potions. And MacGuinness's science-trained mind told him quite clearly that on this planetwide scale the prognosis was likely to be the same one he would give for an individual case: that if the patient was to survive it must be in spite of himself—that he would have to be saved from the consequences of his own ineptitude and given proper treatment. MacGuinness felt a bitter compassion, but he reached for the transmitter switch.

Chapter Ten

Clinical experience to date has only served to confirm the original opinions of Meyer and Klutz that Geo-Nostalgic Psychosis will not yield to any known form of treatment. The only possible course for a Medical Officer under these circumstances is to place the patient under deep sedation. In this respect it should be borne in mind that the condition is so deep-seated and devastating in its mental and physical effects that sedation only serves to slow down the deteriorative process. It is therefore imperative that all possible steps should be taken to ensure the early return of the patient to Earth. Then, and only then, there is a possibility of recovery, and this, if and when it does come, will be due rather to the natural processes than to the effects of any medication.

Corps Medical Handbook:
SURGEON GENERAL KARL HURWITZ

"You can't possibly be serious about this!" Robert Prince stared at his father-in-law, his handsome features frozen in an expression of horror.

"Where an investment of this size is concerned I

am *always* serious," said Elkan Niebohr, seated massively behind his executive desk.

"Have you ever seen a man in the grip of Geonostalgic Psychosis?" said Prince, who sat opposite him in the much less regal chair allocated to visitors.

"No—but I have read accounts."

"Well I *have* seen it," said Prince. "I've seen strong men turned into blubbering, incontinent idiots. One time I was officer on duty when a crewman went raving mad under a sudden attack and fired himself out of one of the missile tubes. A bloody mess."

"My dear Robert, I am just not interested in your horror stories. My mind is made up. All that now remains is to decide which planet we are going to use. In the main there are two requirements—that it should possess approximately Earth gravity, and that it should be, if necessary, expendable."

"Like Koninburger?"

"Now you know very well that is not my attitude at all," said Niebohr with some impatience. "I would hardly be going to so much trouble and expense if I thought so lightly of his survival. Fane's contract alone will cost us a cool two million, apart from the expense of building the underground base for the research project."

"Underground?"

"Naturally. Apart from the fact that it will make the task of preserving Koninburger's illusion that he is still on Earth somewhat easier, it fits in with the story I have told him about the construction of a secret base on the Antarctic continent. He knows very well that Fong would stop his experiments for fear of the dangers outlined by Carter; whereas I have paid him the compliment of telling him that I accept his figures."

"And do you?"

Niebohr spread his hands palms upward on the desk top. "Koninburger is the expert, after all; if he is prepared to risk his own life, who am I to argue with him? And if he succeeds the rewards will be great."

"But if he fails the people at the base will die with him," Prince said. "How does Fane feel about that?"

"Fane's task is to monitor the environment and make sure that Koninburger never for a moment suspects that he is no longer on Earth. It would be of no advantage to him to be burdened with the details of Koninburger's work."

"In other words, you haven't told him of the risk involved," Prince said.

"What would be the point?"

"And the other people who will be working with Koninburger?"

"They will all be specialists, most of them capable of assessing the situation for themselves," Niebohr said. "It's my guess that they will be prepared to accept Koninburger's figures, if only because of the honor of being associated with him in such an historic project."

Prince shook his head, a worried frown on his face. "I can't help but think that the whole operation rests on a very shaky basis—if not an immoral one. Everything depends on maintaining the illusion in the mind of Koninburger that he is still on Earth. If he once has the slightest suspicion, then the whole thing collapses. Apart from anything else, you realize that he could well die as a result? Under the circumstances you might find yourself facing criminal charges."

"You have a lot to learn, Robert," Niebohr said mildly. "I respect your principles and your honesty, but

I must point out that they only represent a point of view—nothing more. Due in some measure to your advice, I have committed the Excelsior Corporation and myself to the development of the Koninburger Drive. I have no intention of backing down now."

"The legal aspect of the matter doesn't bother you at all—the idea that you will be virtually kidnapping Koninburger and transporting him to another system under the influence of drugs?"

"The only real crime in an operation of this magnitude is *failure*," Niebohr said. "Why do you think Fong cornered me for that little heart-to-heart chat the other night? Just to stop Koninburger from experimenting on Earth? Not on your life! If that was all he wanted he could have done it any time he liked."

"Then why?"

"Because Fong knows me well enough to be sure that I wouldn't take such a challenge lying down. United Earth needs that Drive badly, and although there's a chance that Carter and his people on Tarasco IV will come up with the right answers, Fong believes in hedging his bets. He knew that I would find some way of handling the situation that he, in his position, wouldn't dare try. When you're suffering from those occasional pangs of principle, just remember that when he wants a pig killed, even Henry Fong has to go to a butcher." Niebohr rose from his seat and walked across to the left-hand wall of the room, in which was set an enormous, three-dimensional star map on which the zones of the Excelsior Corporation's interests were shown in bright red. "Now then, you're the expert," he said. "Where do we find our expendable, Earth-type planet?"

"Let me have the controls," Prince said. He consulted a table of light years and set the three check rays for the requisite system. He murmured: "You just don't let *anything* stop you, do you?"

"Ah," Niebohr said ironically, "you see it at last, Robert."

"And if it goes bust, you still have the good image from all the favorable publicity, eh?"

"You'll do well as head of the corporation," Niebohr said, "one day."

Chapter Eleven

Then talk not of Inconstancy,
    False Hearts and broken Vows;
If I, by Miracle, can be
This live-long minute true to thee,
    'Tis all that Heav'n allows.

                                        ROCHESTER

Elsa Prince sat on the warm tiles at the side of the kidney-shaped pool smoothing oil onto her deeply tanned body with the delicacy and grace of a cat pursuing its toilet. The process almost complete, she glanced across to the umbrella-shaded table where her father was seated, his hairy belly billowing over the top of a pair of flowered silk shorts, a frosted glass of Campari and soda in his right hand.

"Will it bother you if I take off my bra, Poppa?" she asked.

Niebohr gazed at her fondly, an indulgent smile softening his stony features as he assessed the technical modesty of her bikini, which appeared to consist of little more than two three-centimeter-wide strips of white nylon.

"Why should it? You're built more like a boy, anyway."

"Pig!" she said affectionately, reaching her right hand up behind her back to release the fastening.

The breasts thus revealed were of the same deep reddish-brown color as the rest of her body. Smiling at her father, she proceeded to smooth oil into their firm flesh.

"It's no use your flashing those knockers at me," said Elkan Niebohr with a chuckle. "I changed your diapers, remember?"

"Liar!" she grinned. "You didn't even acknowledge my existence until I was fourteen years old."

"So what are you worried about? Every other male within a thousand miles did, and you must have laid most of them."

"Don't exaggerate, Poppa. I didn't even get to first base with that good-looking company secretary—what was his name—Griefer?"

"Too bad. . ."

"Bothered the hell out of me until one afternoon I found him in bed with your Japanese houseboy," Elsa said reminiscently. "Missionary work never appealed to me."

He sipped his drink, savoring its cool bittersweetness. "You know, sometimes I wonder what you can possibly find to amuse you in a prig like Robert Prince," he said casually.

"One looks for something more than amusement in a husband, Poppa," she said, sitting back and supporting herself on one elbow.

"Such as?"

"Faithfulness and dependability will do for a start."

Niebohr's belly vibrated in another chuckle. "For

God's sake! You talk like an old woman. You're not thirty yet."

"But I *will* be—thirty, forty, fifty—maybe even more. . . And when I am, Bob Prince will still be around."

"And the others?"

"I'll get my share. After all, you still manage."

"I'm a widower," Niebohr pointed out.

"By choice. And anyway, I don't remember you being too exclusive when Belle was alive."

He frowned. "It was that obvious?"

"Perhaps not to other people. But I knew. We're two of a kind, Poppa."

"And Prince—how does he rate for awareness?"

"That's another advantage of being married to an honest man," she said, bringing her knees up to her chin and gazing up at him mockingly from above them. "There's an old French saying: 'A man does not look behind the door unless he has stood there himself.' "

"I learned early not to rely on glib aphorisms," said Niebohr, with a touch of disapproval.

"Maybe so, Poppa, but I tell you this: unless he actually caught me on the job—which I make damned sure he doesn't—Bob would never believe that I had been unfaithful to him."

"But if by some mischance he should find out—what then?" asked Niebohr, genuinely curious.

She shook her head, her delicate hawk-face suddenly serious. "I wouldn't like that, Poppa. I wouldn't like it one bit. You see, I happen to love the guy."

"Love. . ." Niebohr repeated musingly as he raised his glass, marveling at the convolutions of female double-think. Belle had talked a lot about love—for her it had been a tool of reproachful blackmail. To hear the word on Elsa's lips was slightly disturbing.

"You know a Corps officer named Bruce—Tom Bruce?" she said, breaking in on his reflections.

"Sure."

"I met him at the President's place the other night. He's kind of cute."

"That's hardly the description I'd use."

"He and Bob were at Sandpoint together—big buddies."

"Yes, I suppose they would be contemporaries."

"I'm thinking of adding him to my collection."

"Tom Bruce, Commander of *Venturer Twelve*? Now you're really chancing your arm, baby," Niebohr said with a grin. "If anything he's even more stiff-necked and virtuous than Prince."

"Want to bet?" she said, rising suddenly to her feet and walking towards him, her small, perfect body glistening in the sunlight.

"Not against that kind of equipment," he said.

"You knew Bob had offered him the job of Fleet Director, of course?"

"No, as a matter of fact I didn't," Niebohr said.

"Anyway, we've invited Bruce to fly over with us to the Canaries next weekend. Wish me good hunting?"

"I'll do better than that," Niebohr said. "I'll give you a clear field. There's a job that paragon of a husband can do for me out in the Balomain sector—should take him three weeks to a month at least."

She put her arms round his neck and kissed him deliberately on the tip of his beak of a nose. "What a kind, good poppa you are! One of these times you must let me do something nice for you."

"You can do it while you're having your fun," he said, with deadly quietness. "This Bruce—give him the full treatment, spoil him for any other woman, and leave him humiliated—I've seen you do it to men just for kicks. This time do a real job, for *me*."

She looked at him, the cruelty in her dark eyes matching his own. "Maybe you'd like me to castrate him for an encore?" she said.

"I'd like it fine," he said with relish. "Now put those tits away; I'm going to call for another drink."

In the early hours of the following morning the insistent beeping of his bedside vidphone roused him from his sleep. Instantly alert, he raised himself into a sitting position and punched the button.

"Perez, Communications Section, here, sir," said the dark-haired young man whose face appeared in the screen. "I'm sorry to disturb you at this time, but a Triple A Emergency message just came through from Orphelin Three addressed to you personally."

"Who sent it?" demanded Niebohr.

"Professor MacGuinness, sir."

"That blasted Scotch fish-fancier. Now what the hell could be so urgent with him?"

Perez went a shade paler. "I wouldn't know, sir. The message is in code."

"So don't sit there apologizing—shoot me a copy right away!" roared Niebohr, launching his bulk off the bed.

"Yes, sir."

The fax slot at the base of the phone hummed briefly and began to extrude a band of paper covered with dense upper-case type. The band was about a meter long by the time the phone clucked briefly and the process stopped.

Niebohr, swathed in a bright-scarlet silk dressing gown bent down and picked up the paper; as he did so he became aware of the scrutiny of Perez's nervous eyes.

"Well?"

"I was wondering what you wanted me to do with the original, sir."

Niebohr told him, then punched the button to clear the screen.

He walked out of the bedroom into a small, well-equipped private office, where he fed the length of paper into the scanner of an already programmed decoder.

Within less than thirty seconds the translated message, now printed on pale-green paper, began to unwind from the machine. He waited impatiently until the process was completed, then picked up the paper and took it across to his desk, where he sat down to read through it.

Three minutes later, his face dark with rage, he activated his desk vidphone. "Get me Foster!" he shouted as soon as the face of the building's night operator appeared on the screen.

"Foster, Mr. Niebohr?" said the startled girl, her mouth wide open as she stared at the apparition.

"George Foster—Head of Ecology Section."

"Sir. . .I don't know. . ." The girl's flustered hands grabbed at the ends of her frizzy blonde hair. "I mean. . ."

"You should find his home number on your emergency directory," said Niebohr. "I want his face on this screen within five minutes, understand?"

"Well, I'll try, sir, but. . ."

"Too damned right, you'll try," roared Niebohr. "If you don't make it, you'll be back tomorrow peddling your arse on fourth-level Bastown."

Rising from behind the desk, he went back into the

bedroom and began to get dressed. There would be no more sleep for him this night.

George Foster was a small sandy-haired man with sharp features and a nervous tic, which caused the end of his long nose to twitch in moments of stress. The ratlike nose was quivering now, as he looked up from his perusal of the decoded MacGuinness message into the looming, angry visage of his employer.

"Well? Is he right?" demanded Niebohr.

Foster eased a sliver of pink tongue over his dry lips. "I wouldn't like to commit myself without access to all the data, but bearing in mind MacGuinness's reputation. . ."

"I hired him on your recommendation."

"As I was saying, bearing in mind MacGuinness's reputation, it seems very likely that he may be right. This parallel between the bio-clock acceleration effect on fish and humans appears to be a valid one. . ."

"Then why in hell didn't your people spot it?"

"With due respect, sir, I did draw your attention to the acceleration of maturation processes in Orphelin-born children, suggesting at the time that a certain reduction of life-span might be expected as a result. A figure of twenty percent was mentioned, I believe—one that you yourself declared acceptable. However, if the process is a progressive one. . ."

"Then what?"

"One hesitates to be dogmatic in such matters," said Foster, obviously trying to choose his words carefully. "We already know that children of the first Orphelin-conceived generation reach puberty at around the age of 7 years, so that some of them have married and had their own children at the age of 10. And, as MacGuinness has pointed out, the maturation of this second generation appears to be even more precocious, attaining maturity in some cases at least a year earlier. If he is correct in drawing a parallel with the fish situation, the mutation will not have run its full course and become stabilized until perhaps ten or fifteen generations."

"And when it does become stabilized?" said Niebohr.

Foster's entire face twitched unhappily. "It seems to me quite likely that MacGuinness's estimate may be right, and the life expectancy of a human being on Orphelin Three—or more correctly, as he suggests, the new sub-species *homo sapiens (Orphelis)*—will be considerably reduced, the individual being born, growing up into a brief adulthood, and descending into senility within the space of twelve years."

"You realize that the Orphelin colony is due for its twenty-five-year checkover by Colonization Commission experts in eighteen months time?" said Niebohr.

Foster nodded. "That had occurred to me, sir."

"Do you think there's a chance they might miss this thing?" said Niebohr. "After all, you said yourself that as yet it is nowhere near to having run its course. If MacGuinness were gagged. . ."

"Mr. Niebohr, the detection of this kind of thing is precisely the job of the Colonization Commission people—their whole training is oriented in such fields. Perhaps if you had been more cautious in the first instance, instead of rushing into the Orphelin project on the basis of a very sketchy preliminary report. . ."

"Don't try to second-guess me, Foster!" roared Niebohr. "The decision I took was right at the time—without it there would be no Excelsior Corporation as it exists today."

"I can only agree with you there," said Foster. "But

what of the future? The repercussions are sure to be very damaging for the corporation—and as the leading figure in the project, the consequences for you personally—"

"*If* the situation becomes known," said Niebohr.

Foster spread his quivering hands. "But how can you possibly prevent it?"

Niebohr picked up the long sheet of pale-green paper containing MacGuinness's decoded message and began to tear it methodically to shreds. Afterwards, as Foster watched, he placed it in an ashtray and sprayed it with flame from his desk cigar lighter.

"There's always a way—there *has* to be," he said, crumbling the ashes to grey powder with his large fingers. Tight-lipped, he inhaled deeply. Yes, there was always a solution; there was one here. Without the flicker of a moral consideration, a plan began to form in his mind.

Chapter Twelve

In skating over thin ice, our safety is in our speed.

EMERSON

"I fail to see that a few days is going to make much difference," said Robert Prince, frowning. "For one thing, Elsa and I have a number of people joining us for the weekend on Hierro."

Niebohr's hooded eyes regarded his son-in-law sardonically across the dinner table. "By God, the old Corps training soon rubs off, doesn't it? I can hardly imagine you making a speech like that to Admiral Carter if he ordered you off on an expedition to hell-and-gone at five minutes notice."

"That's not the point," said Prince. "In such a case the situation would be an emergency, and there would be a fully equipped and crewed ship on standby."

"*Medusa* is ready and waiting for liftoff at eight hundred tomorrow morning—all the necessary equipment and personnel will be aboard tonight."

"I gave no such orders, and I'm supposed to be Fleet Director," Prince said.

"But *I* did," Niebohr said, helping himself to another wedge of Camembert.

Prince, his face very pale, turned to Elsa, who had been sitting quietly at the head of the table toying with a long-stemmed glass of red wine. "Elsa, perhaps you can make your father understand that I detest the way he gives me authority with one hand and takes it back with the other."

"Now, darling," Elsa said gently, smiling across at him. "I'm sure Poppa has his own very good reasons for doing what he has done. I never knew him when he didn't."

"That is not the point. . ."

"No, of course it isn't," Elsa said. "The real crux of the matter is that your pride has been hurt, and I agree with you. But that's the way Poppa is—you should know by now that he's as subtle as a bulldozer."

Prince looked from father to daughter and had a sudden uneasy feeling that he was being manipulated in some way. It was quite out of character for Elsa to accept the implied ruin of her plans without some form of protest—and even Elkan Niebohr had been known to quail before her rage.

"You don't mind about the weekend?" he asked.

Elsa thrust the glass to one side. "Of course I mind, but I know better than to argue with Poppa when he's made a decision. After all, there'll be other weekends. You know, I suddenly feel rather tired. I think I'll go up." She stood and stretched herself like a well-fed cat, then walked over and kissed her father on the top of his bald head. "Goodnight, super-pig," she purred. "And don't keep my husband up late; I've got something that needs his attention."

Treating Prince to a cheeky grin, she camped outrageously out of the room.

"You know, sometimes I wonder if you realize what a lucky young bastard you are," said Elkan Niebohr, wiping his hands on his napkin and rising to his feet. "Come on, let's try some of that Carlos Tercero brandy Gonzales sent me last week. . .and talk this thing over sensibly."

Moving to the sideboard, he poured two generous measures into balloon glasses and handed one to Prince. Then he stood with his back to the large open fireplace, warming the glass with his palms as he looked at his son-in-law.

"You may have noticed that in the usual course of events I don't explain my decisions," he said benevolently. "But in your case, just this once, I'll make an exception. There are several reasons for my apparent haste in this matter. For one thing, Koninburger is becoming impatient. He had me on the vid for a whole half hour today demanding that I give him the facilities he needs to carry on with his work. . .I think he has some idea that Carter and his people may be getting ahead of him."

"And are they?"

"My reports are that the Tarasco experimental base isn't in operation yet," said Niebohr. "But it can only be a matter of weeks before it is. Bear in mind that we have a big construction job on our hands even when we've settled on a location."

"I thought we already had. The rock on Balomain is soft and workable, according to our reports."

Niebohr bent his hawk-nose over the contents of his glass and sniffed appreciatively. "Maybe so, but I'm beginning to wonder if it isn't a mite too far away for our purpose. I've been considering Orphelin Four as a possible alternative. For one thing, it would be much easier from the supply point of view—a lot of the necessary stuff could be shipped across from Orphelin Three, just a local hop."

"Aren't you forgetting about that fifty percent methane atmosphere?"

Niebohr shrugged. "As the base will be underground, and a completely self-contained environmental unit, I don't see that as an important objection. Anyway, it's always a good idea to have some kind of alternative in a deal of this kind, so I've decided to hedge my bets."

"Like how?"

"I've had a medium-sized scout ship located aboard *Medusa,* complete with a five-man crew and ten more experts. You can take *Medusa* to Balomain via the Orphelin system, dropping off Wernher's party there and collecting them again on your way back to Earth."

"Wernher—that thug? I never knew that he was a construction expert," said Prince.

"He isn't—but somebody has to be in charge, and he can do the job as well as anybody."

Prince sipped the fiery brandy, trying to guess what was going on beneath that great, domed skull. Sometimes he found himself wondering if Gould and some of the others weren't right in their covert suggestions that the Old Man's taste for autocratic decisions had already slipped over the brink into megalomania.

"All right, Poppa, if that's the way you want it," he said at length. "Just one thing—I hope you've told that ape Wernher to keep out of my way."

"My dear Robert, there's no reason whatever for you to have any fears on that score," Niebohr said, smiling. "I've made it quite clear to him that he, the scout ship, and the men aboard it are strictly cargo as far as you are concerned. They have instructions to keep themselves entirely to themselves. And I might suggest that you do the same. There's no point in lousing up an operation like this by harking back to past quarrels. Do I make myself clear?"

"Completely," said Prince. "Any further instructions?"

"No—your construction experts and geologists have already been fully briefed on what is required," Niebohr said. "All you need to do is act as bus driver for them."

"In that case I'll bid you goodnight," Prince said stiffly. He placed his still-half-full glass of brandy on a table and began to walk towards the door of the room. He was almost there when he heard Niebohr's voice call his name.

"Robert!"

He turned to see the old man standing, enormous and gargoyle-like, in the flickering light of the open fireplace.

"Yes?"

"Don't take it out on Elsa," said Niebohr. "I wouldn't like that."

Chapter Thirteen

. . . at 90% of his full salary at the time of retirement, plus the usual yearly cost-of-living increments. However, should the said officer be convicted of any misconduct or neglect of his proper duties, the amount of the above-mentioned pension may be reduced at the discretion of the Board. In such cases it is recommended that . . .

Extract from EXCELSIOR COLONIZATION CORPORATION STANDARD CONTRACT FOR OFFICERS

Charles Coogan, first officer of the *Medusa*, cursed his luck as the ramrod-straight figure of Robert Prince appeared through the door at the other end of the ship's control section. A heavily-built man, with a decided paunch and the bulbous reddish features of a steady drinker, Chuck Coogan was looking forward to his retirement in six months' time. His illusions about the romance of merchant-spacing had died early, and for the past fifteen years he had cherished a simple dream involving a place in the sun, a beach, and plenty of cheap booze. A woman? Maybe. . .a very big maybe. He had tried the marriage bit a couple of times, but the life of a spacer was tough on to-getherness—no reasonably attractive woman was going to spend maybe nine tenths of her life sleeping alone, even if she did have the consolation of a comfortable monthly check. No—the bottle was better. On that a guy could rely.

Provided nothing happened to stop the flow of that steady fifteen thousand credits a year, plus increments. . . Nothing like a bad report to the Board from that cocky young ex-Corps whiz kid, who was right now walking along past the ratings at the control consoles, his goddamned hawk-eyes checking everything from sewage disposal to drive frequency. Coogan bent over the tri-di tank, star-map simulator, an expression of concentration on his heavy features. At his age, after a lifetime of hard service and little reward, surely a guy deserved a better break than to be saddled with a niggling young bastard like Prince on what would probably be Coogan's last trip?

The small white hairs at the back of his neck seemed to act as antennae, sensing the approach; but even so, the voice when it came made him start nervously.

"Good afternoon, Mr. Coogan. Your report, please."

Chuck wheeled, throwing up a sloppy salute. Hell! Merchant commanders didn't usually bother with that kind of thing, but this young upstart with his fancy Corps ideas insisted on all the trimmings. All the more galling when you considered that he'd got the job of Fleet Director more on the strength of his screwing ability than anything else.

"Mr. Coogan?" The expression in Prince's alert blue eyes made Chuck suddenly aware of the sloppiness of his own crumpled uniform and the perfunctory nature of the shave he had taken that morning.

"All's well, sir. We're two hours ahead of schedule as of the last course check. ETA in the Orphelin system 16.00 hours Earth Standard tomorrow."

"Very good, Mr. Coogan. Carry on with your duties." The salute was returned with Sandpoint precision and Prince turned away to continue his inspection.

Coogan watched him move away down the line, relaxing slightly in the growing assurance that he had survived yet another encounter. He glanced at the master clock. Only fifty more minutes to go of this watch before he could head for the security of his cabin and the consolation of a shot—no, several shots —of good bourbon. He turned back to his study of the star map.

"Mr. Coogan!" The voice called—this time with an unmistakable edge.

Hell! What now? He looked up to see Prince standing some three meters away, one hand pointing to a bank of dials.

"Sir?" He shambled forward.

"Are you aware of the state of the radioactivity count in the main aft hold?" demanded Prince.

Chuck, who *wasn't* so aware, craned forward to look and saw that the dial was ten points up on normal. Momentary panic was soothed by a sudden fortunate inspiration.

"Yes, sir," he said. "If you will recall, that is where the scout ship bound for the Orphelin system is stowed."

"I'm well aware of that, Mr. Coogan," Prince said coldly. "But I fail to see how it accounts for the situation."

"Well, sir, I figured that there was maybe a slight residual leak from the scout's secondaries," improvised Coogan plausibly.

"Then there shouldn't be," Prince said indignantly. "A scout ship carried as hold cargo should be on full shut-down, with no leakages. That is clearly laid down in regulations. Apart from anything else, have you considered the possible radiation hazard to any crew members working in that hold?"

"There's nobody down there, sir," Coogan said. "If you recall, your instructions were quite specific that the hold should remain sealed throughout the voyage."

"I'm well aware of my instructions," Prince said with an air of tired patience that implied he was talking to an idiot. "But what about the party aboard the scout ship? Is their safety not to be considered?"

"Well, sir, I. . ." Chuck's voice trailed away hopelessly. Didn't matter what effort a guy made, you couldn't win with a punctilious bastard like Prince. "You want I should go down there and check it out?"

"No, Mr. Coogan. Your place, as you very well know, is here on the bridge," Prince said. "*I* will attend to this matter personally."

Chuck Coogan stood by the incorruptible radiation indicator, swearing with quiet, concentrated venom as the tall figure in the immaculate uniform marched briskly away and disappeared through the doorway.

"Why the fancy dress, Bobbie?" asked Kurt Werner, who had stood in the open main airlock of the scout ship watching Prince's progress across the deck of the hold with a derisive grin on his face.

"I see nothing humorous in the idea of my taking

precautionary measures," said Robert Prince, who was wearing a radiation suit and carrying a portable counter. "The ship's monitoring system shows radioactivity in this hold as ten points above normal."

"You don't say," said Wernher contemptuously. "So what happens now, we all start sprouting extra heads or something?"

This witticism was received appreciatively by the audience—half a dozen tough-looking characters in black coveralls, who had stopped their game of craps to watch the encounter. Unlikely as it seemed, Prince assumed that they must be members of Wernher's team of engineers and geologists.

"What happens now," he said firmly, "is that I come aboard that ship and pinpoint the radiation source, after which I shall take steps to remove the hazard."

"Sorry, Bobbie, I'm afraid I can't let you do that." Wernher shook his dark, close-cropped head from side to side as he remained stationary, effectively blocking Prince's passage.

"You can't stop me," Prince said. "As captain of this ship I am responsible for the safety of her cargo and personnel. I have the authority to carry out any inspection I consider necessary to this purpose."

"You do? Well that's really interesting," Wernher said, still grinning. "But you're not coming aboard this scout ship."

"I warn you that you will be contravening Merchant Spacer regulations if you try to prevent me," Prince said.

"Yes, and I bet you know the bloody page-number and paragraph involved," Wernher said contemptuously. "Come off it, Bobbie! You're not in the Corps now, so you can stop giving me the old stiff-upper-lip treatment. In case you'd forgotten, we're both working for Excelsior, and I am under direct orders from Niebohr. You want to make any inspection of this ship, you get permission from the Old Man himself."

Prince took a firm grip on his rising anger. "I can't understand why you're being so unreasonable about this, Wernher. It's in the interests of everyone aboard —and particularly these men of yours—that this radiation should be stopped."

"The way I hear it, ten points is still way below the danger level," Wernher said. "So why all the panic? If you were wearing a couple of luminous wrist watches you'd be in about the same amount of hazard."

"Any radiation is a potential source of danger until it has been assessed and fully inspected to ensure that there is no chance of a sudden increase in its intensity—"

"Boy! I bet that was right out of the book, word for word, wasn't it?" Wernher said. "Well let me tell you this, Bobbie—then maybe you'll stop peeing in your drawers—there just ain't no way that radiation source could step itself up, unless we wanted it to. We're going down to Orphelin Four to make a survey of the possibilities of building an underground base, right? Now you may be big stuff as a space captain, but you obviously don't know a damned thing about geological and seismological investigations of this kind, otherwise you'd realize that we have to carry a certain amount of blasting equipment."

"Assuming that to be the case," Prince said stubbornly, "there is clearly some fault in the shielding of this equipment, and I must still insist that you respect my authority—"

"You just don't listen, do you?" said Wernher. Slipping his right hand into the side pocket of his coveralls with apparent casualness, he brought it out again immediately carrying a small deadly needler.

"What do you think you're doing?" demanded Prince.

"I am showing you *my* authority," Wernher said. The grin was gone from his face now, and his voice was flat and deadly. "And don't you think it wouldn't give me a great deal of pleasure to use it. Now piss off! Before I tell the boys here to rough you up a little."

White-faced and quivering with rage, Prince turned abruptly on his heel and walked out of the hold. Wernher would pay for his insolence when they eventually got back to Earth, he was determined on that, but for the time being he was forced to recognize that he could do nothing. They were under Niebohr's orders. Prince tried to swallow the bitter truth that, even though he was millions of miles away, his father-in-law was still in command.

Chapter Fourteen

> *Man is a creature of extremes, capable of godlike acts of self-sacrifice or devilish cruelties of self-interest. In either of these roles he is likely to be motivated by completely subjective reasoning.*
>
> THE WIT AND WISDOM OF HENRY FONG
> (p. 234)

Angus MacGuinness stood on the grassy bank in the bright sunlight looking down into the broken mirror of the swift-flowing, gravel-bottomed shallows. The water was boiling with fish—the males, hump-backed with great enlarged jaws and doglike teeth, escorting the females heavy with spawn as they scooped out saucer-like depressions with flapping movements of body and tail, and engaging occasionally in formalized combats with other males who approached too close to the redds. The cruel joy of the reproductive process was one that never failed to impress him with its special mystery, with its implication of forces that Man, for all his apparent civilization and knowledge, was only partially capable of comprehending.

On this occasion the solemn impression went even

deeper into MacGuinness's consciousness because of his recent reminder that those same forces were at work on Man, shaping his destiny, the very stuff of his life, in unguessable ways. The two stocky, grey-haired men who stood one on either side of him were each in his own way victims—or playthings—of those forces, although at this time neither had any knowledge of the fact. MacGuinness, warm in his regard for these men who had begun as mere hired helpers and were now two valued and respected friends, had not yet found the courage to tell them what he had discovered, to explain to them that the planet they both loved as their home was in fact a beautiful trap. The discovery had been his, but the responsibility for what must be done about it must lie—he thanked his Agnostic God—in other hands.

"You all right, Professor?"

MacGuinness jerked out of his self-examination to find himself staring into the weatherbeaten, middle-aged face of the twenty-two-year-old Alan Emery.

"I'm just fine, Alan," he said, the other's concern kindling yet another twinge of guilt at his own inadequacy in the situation.

"You're sure?" The wrinkles on Alan's face deepened in concern. "We've both been kind of worried about you lately. You don't seem to talk quite so much as you used."

"Och! We're a black lot, we MacGuinnesses, with moods that change like the highland winds," said MacGuinness, forcing a smile. "You must not make too much notice of my funny ways."

"Bill and I were wondering if it might not be a good idea to take a few days off," Alan said. "We could all go over to the mainland for a while—Josiah-town, perhaps. There's plenty to do and see there that you must have missed when you arrived and left in such a hurry to see your fishes."

Josiahtown was a bustling, brash, prosperous new city with a population of over a quarter-million happy, hard-working people, people who carried in their loins the seed that would condemn their descendants to the creeping doom of a gradually decreasing life-expectancy. All those as yet unknown faces, those eyes to be looked into—and he carrying the burden of this knowledge. . .

"No, I think I'd best stay here for a while yet," said MacGuinness. "At least until this breeding run is finished."

Alan Emery shrugged. "All right, Professor—you're the boss. I was—" He stopped in mid-sentence, looking down at the ground. "Did you feel that?"

"I did," said Bill. "It was as if the island trembled beneath my feet."

MacGuinness had felt it too—a deep, shuddering vibration that went on for maybe five seconds, boring frighteningly into the depths of his body.

"Earthquake?" he said. "Or volcanic activity of some kind?"

Bill Emery frowned. "Not in my experience," he said. "According to the experts, the planetary crust settled finally more than half a million years before we came on the scene."

"Nevertheless, I think we'll take a look," said MacGuinness, turning his back on the spawning beds and striding through the lush grass towards their camp.

Inside the hut he stared at the instruments. "This is stupid," MacGuinness said. "I've got a mess of P, L and S waves all at once. According to this, the earthquake started at ground level and then went down to—good God!"

Fear of the unknown touched the faces of Mac-Guinness's helpers. "What's that mean?" Bill asked.

It was possibly only imagination that made the biologist's whiskers seem to bristle. "Nought to sixty kilometers is normal, sixty to two hundred is intermediate, two hundred and fifty is deep. But the isoseismal lines say this *penetrated* to five hundred and eighty kilometers below ground level."

The sound of the waves came distantly; the cry of seabirds seemed to echo the waves.

"What's this dial?" Alan asked.

"The Richter magnitude register," MacGuinness said, disbelief showing in his concentration and alarm. "It's stuck at ten, which is two more strengths than theoretically possible without partial break-up of the planet." He glared at another dial. "And the bloody Marcalli scale there agrees with it. And that's not all. Focus and epicenter seem to be one and the same thing. Some earthquake!"

"You mean it's not an earthquake?" Bill Emery was clenching and unclenching his fists.

"Oh no, I won't say that. But this quiet little planet of yours seems to have its own special brand of upheaval."

"Will we have tidal waves?"

"No. If I'm any judge—and this certainly is not my field—the great ocean and the island chains will be in the shadow zone. Around the Tantaron continent, it may not be so. Your seismologists are going to have to revise their ideas, that's certain."

Bill Emery's face was deadly serious. "It's the buildings I'm more concerned with right now," he said. "Some of those high-rise apartment buildings in Josiahtown are pretty flimsy to take that kind of treatment."

"Anne Marie and the kids!" exclaimed Alan.

"That's who I was thinking about," Bill said. "I think we'd better check on just what has happened." He hurried out of the instrument hut at a run, with Alan following close behind.

By the time MacGuinness reached the flycar, Bill was in the pilot seat, the radio mike in his hand, repeating: "Josiahtown Central, Josiahtown Central, do you read me? Josiahtown Central. . ."

Five minutes later Bill abandoned the fruitless effort. He looked up at MacGuinness, fear peering out of his eyes.

"Nothing—not a damned thing," he said. "Not even any of the commercial stations on the air. Surely an earthquake couldn't be that bad?"

MacGuinness felt a dreadful premonition of disaster moving in on his mind like a dark cloud. "I think we'd better go and take a look," he said quietly.

The completeness of the devastation became obvious as soon as they crossed the continental coastline, but it seemed to increase in its intensity as they moved inland toward Josiahtown. After their initial expressions of surprise they flew on in grim silence over the blackened, carbonized ruins of once-fertile farmlands and forests, searching in vain for any signs of life, either animal or human.

For a long time the only sound apart from the hum of the flycar's engine was the wild chattering of the radiation counter on the control panel. At last MacGuinness found the courage to speak of what he knew must be in the minds of the others.

"Ye'll have realized that it's no earthquake that did this," he said, his voice tight and angry. "I've never seen the like of it, except in some old film records dating back to the nineteen hundreds, and I never expected to see it again."

"A nuclear bomb," breathed Bill Emery.

"I'd guess *bombs,* rather," MacGuinness said. "I've detected two distinct epicenters already. I'd say it was a multiple war-head missile, with the kind of spread that would enable it to sterilize the entire continent."

"And Josiahtown?"

"As the main center of population it would clearly be a prime target," MacGuinness said.

"God!" Alan Emery groaned and slumped forward in his seat, head in hands, sobbing uncontrollably.

"When you say sterilization. . . ?" queried Bill.

"A calculated destruction of all forms of life." Mac-Guinness glanced worriedly at the radiation counter. "I don't know just how good the shielding is on this flycar, but I think we should be turning back any time now."

"No!" shouted Alan, straightening up, his face wild with grief. "We must go on. I have to find Anne Marie."

MacGuinness shook his head. "It's no good, laddie. Even if anybody survived the initial blast and heat, they'd still be as good as dead with this kind of fall-out. There would be nothing we could do to help them."

"You mean *everybody?*" Bill said.

"If not at this moment, then certainly within twenty-four hours. We three will be the only people alive on Orphelin Three," said MacGuinness, "unless we commit suicide by carrying on in what must be a fruitless search."

"That's good enough for me," said Bill, putting the flycar into a sharp turn and heading back toward the coast in spite of Alan's protestations. "There's just one thing that bothers me, Professor."

"Yes?"

"If we really are the only survivors, what do we go on living for?"

"Revenge, perhaps?" said MacGuinness.

"Against an enemy who hops back into sub-space?"

"We'll catch up," said MacGuinness. "The fact that we know it can be done puts us at least twenty-five percent of the way along the road to our sub-space drive."

"And meantime the list grows—Minos IV, Kepler III, and now—us. Orphelin III."

"Aye, the Kilroys will have a lot to answer for when the Corps finally do catch up with them," said MacGuinness, looking down at the blackened, desolate landscape.

"I heard somewhere once that they probably don't think of us as intelligent beings at all," said Bill musingly.

"Then the sooner we start hitting back the better," said MacGuinness. He glanced worriedly at Alan, whose protestations and tears had now died down into complete silence. He was sitting, shoulders slumped forward, staring ahead with dull, unseeing eyes, in a withdrawn state.

"Back to the island?" said Bill as they approached the coastline again.

"Where else?" said MacGuinness. "Provided the radioactivity doesn't drift too quickly in that direction, we should be safe enough for a few days, at least."

"And after that?"

"The communications blackout is sure to bring the Corps running," said MacGuinness. "And they're sure to give the entire planet a thorough checkover for survivors. We'll activate the flycar's emergency beacon in a few days' time. They'll pick us up, all right."

"And you'll be headed back to Earth," said Bill. "Even if the fish do survive the radioactivity, there'll be no one around to run the industry, no one to. . ." his voice choked, then recovered slightly. "Two of us—two, out of five million people. Do you think they'll send more colonists out here, when the effects of the fallout die down?"

"I expect so," said MacGuinness. "But that will be some time yet. There'll have to be an entire new survey to check on safety." A survey of the kind that should have been made in the first instance, but clearly never was—one that would go deep into the causes of the progeric mutation and search for some method of counteracting its effects. Without such a remedy there could be no possibility of sending new colonists, even if United Earth were willing to put more human beings at risk in what must now be regarded as a Kilroy area.

Chapter Fifteen

For we know they must be there
Out beyond the reach of drive and mind.
We have seen their footprints in the stars,
Those
Other
Men. . .

Kilroy: IVAN KAVANIN

It was late afternoon when MacGuinness and his companions arrived back at the island. Alan Emery was still in his withdrawn, shocked state to such an extent that the biologist and Bill practically had to carry him out of the flycar and into the hut. Once there, they laid him on his cot and MacGuinness gave him a sedative injection, which soon put him to sleep.

"Och, it'll be the best thing for him," said MacGuinness. "When he wakes up tomorrow morning the trauma will already be well on the way towards healing."

"I wonder. . ." Bill said thoughtfully. "He's always been pretty much of an extroverted type, letting emotion go the way it would. This thing has hit him pretty hard, and I'm afraid he isn't going to come out of it that easy."

"The Corps medics will be able to help him when they arrive. They're used to handling this sort of condition," said MacGuinness, hating his own glibness as he mouthed the words. What psyche-treatment could possibly make up for the kind of loss these two men had suffered, or counteract the shattering knowledge that they were the last remaining survivors of their society? The thought reminded him that at this stage survival was by no means a certainty, conditional as it was on a Corps rescue party reaching them before the prevailing winds swept the plague of radioactive contamination south over the islands.

"How long do you think it will be before the Corps arrive?" said Bill Emery, as if catching the echo of his thought.

"I'm not quite sure what the routine procedure is in this kind of thing," MacGuinness said, scratching in the black depths of his beard. "But I'd guess three days at most from the time Excelsior reports the communications blackout—and they're not going to drag their heels. The Corporation has too much at stake here on Orphelin Three—or rather *had.* . . Old Man Niebohr is going to set up a real howl about this, you can rely on that. One thing for sure, he'll blame what has happened just as much on Corps inefficiency as he does on the Kilroys. He's not going to lose an opportunity like this."

"I suppose in that case the five million people who died here didn't do so in vain," said Bill Emery. "They will at least make a political point for Mr. Niebohr."

MacGuinness looked helplessly at the colonist, shocked by the flat bitterness of his tone and yet recognizing its justification. What did the destruction of five million people on a planet light-years distant really mean to them back on Earth? The whole thing would seem unimaginably remote to the average man on the walkway—even more so because President Fong in his wisdom had decreed that any news of the activities of the Kilroys should be carefully diluted, for fear of causing a panic reaction.

He glanced across at the sleeping, defenseless figure of Alan Emery and was once again reminded of that other hazard that had hung over Orphelin Three. Alan at least stood a good chance of living out his natural life-span, but whose was the responsibility for the fact that that life would be foreshortened by thirty or forty years? There was another reckoning to be considered on his return to Earth—one of which he must not lose sight.

It seemed to him that he had a direct obligation to obtain recognition and justice for the survivors— and the dead—of Orphelin Three.

He and Bill Emery ate a silent meal without relish. Neither of them had the heart to make social conversation, and even less to talk about the matters that were really on their minds. Afterwards MacGuinness lit one of his cigars and walked out of the hut, as was his usual custom before retiring to his bed. The sight of the great dome of stars visible through the unpolluted atmosphere of Orphelin Three was one that never failed to impress him with a special kind of awe. Tonight there was a new, frightening undercurrent to that awe, a freshly awakened awareness of his own vulnerability, a reminder of the fact that he was a tiny, ant-like creature staring up into a hostile universe, which might at any time choose to obliterate him and all his kind.

Ashamed of his own cowardice, he sought the shelter of the hut once again. Bill Emery was already in bed, his face turned to the wall, and Alan was deep in his drug-induced sleep. MacGuinness undressed quietly and got into his own bed. He lay awake for a long time in the darkness before sleep finally came, and when it did there was little release in its nature, filled as it was with echoes of the dreadful images of the shattered, blackened landscapes of Orphelin Three.

It was full daylight when MacGuinness awoke, clawing his way out of sleep with a breathless moan of terror. He sat up and found that he was alone in the hut. From outside he could hear the sound of Bill's voice calling.

Startled by the urgency of the sound, he paused only to slip on his shoes and ran out into the sunlight stark naked. Bill was standing, one arm raised in a helpless gesture towards the flycar, which was already some twenty meters high and heading with growing speed away from the island.

"What happened?" demanded MacGuinness.

Bill turned to reveal a fast-growing bruise on the side of his jaw. "I woke up to find Alan gone," he explained. "When I came out of the hut he was just getting aboard the flycar, babbling and talking to himself, delirious. Something about going home to Anne Marie, and a lot of other stuff. I caught him by the shoulder and asked him what he was doing. He turned and looked at me as if he'd never seen me before in his life. Then he clobbered me. I'm sorry, Professor; I should have stopped him."

"What more could you have done?" said MacGuinness.

"I could have saved him—at least him, my own son," Bill said brokenly, his eyes filling with sudden tears.

MacGuinness averted his eyes from the distressing sight, looking up into the bright morning sky. The flycar was already several kilometers north of the island and there was absolutely nothing either of them could do to bring it back. Alan would end his already foreshortened life within a few hours, victim of the same bombs that had killed the rest of his people. There was no—

MacGuinness let out a sudden whoop of excitement and grabbed at Bill Emery's shoulder. "Look, man, look!" he yelled, pointing upwards into the northwest, where the dark, unmistakable shape of a fast-pursuit copter was rushing across the sky on an interception course with the flycar.

"Thank God!" said Bill Emery. "There must have been a Corps ship right here in the system—or at least very near by."

"Aye, we're saved," said MacGuinness, suddenly conscious of his nakedness for the first time. "I'd better go in and put some clothes on before our visitors arrive—they have mixed crews on those Corps ships."

He turned to hurry away, but he had only gone a couple of paces when Bill's voice made him stop and wheel around.

"The bastards! The rotten, murdering bastards!" yelled Bill, shaking his fists impotently at the sky.

The flycar containing Alan Emery fell toward the ocean, wreathed in a ball of flame. The sound of the explosion reached them a moment later, as the flame disappeared beneath the surface.

"They shot him down—in cold blood!" said Bill. "Why? Why would they do a thing like that?"

MacGuinness looked upwards. The copter had changed its course now and was heading purposefully toward the island on which they were standing.

"Because that's no rescue team—it's a mopping up squad!" he shouted. "Come on—let's get out of here!"

Pausing only to grab a hunting rifle that stood near the door of the hut, MacGuinness half-dragged the still-stunned Bill Emery out of the camp and into the cover of the wood which stood on the hillside behind. Thorny bushes slashed at his unprotected flesh, but it was only when they were well into the woods that he looked down at his bloodied, naked body and realized what had happened. For the moment, at least, the adrenalin pumping through his system left him unconscious of any pain. He laid the rifle down and leaned against a tree, gulping down air and listening to the thundering of his own heart.

"They're landing!" said Bill.

MacGuinness turned and looked down toward the camp. The copter was a plain dark green, with no identification markings. As he watched, it settled to the ground and a door in its side slid open. Half a dozen humanoid figures, wearing lightweight white radiation suits and carrying hand weapons, leapt out and scattered through the buildings of the camp with the efficiency of highly trained guerrillas.

"And they're looking for us," said MacGuinness. "Make no mistake about that. . . Do you realize we're probably the first human beings who ever saw a party of Kilroys in the flesh? Strange, but there doesn't seem anything unlikely in the fact that they turn out to be humanoid in general shape. After all, if we are Man, then they are surely Anti-Man, and there would surely be. . ." MacGuinness stopped himself talking deliberately as he became aware that what he was really doing was merely babbling to relieve his panic. "Sorry, Bill, I. . ." He turned to apologize—but his companion and the rifle were gone.

There was a hint of movement in the undergrowth several meters down the hillside, but no certain sight of Bill. Down in the camp, the instrument and the supply huts were already in flames. Weaponless and naked, MacGuinness could only stand and watch.

The mopping-up party was moving in on the larger living hut now in a tightening cordon. One of them was almost at the open doorway when Bill Emery burst out of the undergrowth at the bottom of the hill, screaming his hatred and firing the hunting rifle.

The humanoid nearest the doorway of the hut wheeled and dropped his weapon as he lurched back into the dimness of the interior and out of MacGuinness's sight. Still howling like a madman, Bill loosed one. . .two more shots at the other members of the squad before a hail of returning fire smashed him to the ground.

After that it was merely a matter of routine destruction. Two of the humanoids helped their wounded companion back to the copter, while another of their number dragged Bill Emery's body into the main hut. Soon the hut and its contents were burning fiercely, but it appeared that even the destruction by the flames was not sufficient for the aliens' purposes. Two of them carried a large object about the size of a ten-gallon oil drum and placed it in the dead center of the camp. MacGuinness watched as one of them bent to make adjustments to some controls on the side of the object, then straightened up to call something unintelligible to the other members of the party, who all hurried to board the copter again in response.

Thirty seconds later the machine was airborne again and heading swiftly away from the island. MacGuinness guessed that the aliens had placed some kind of demolition charge calculated to remove all traces of the camp, now that they had presumably eliminated its inhabitants. He turned and hurried away into the undergrowth.

By the time the explosion happened he was over the brow of the hill, in open grassland dotted with an occasional clump of bushes. The sound of the copter had already faded to a distant rumble.

He stood naked and bloody in the sunlight, suddenly burdened by the awareness that he was the only human being left alive on Orphelin Three. A human being stripped of all the aids of his civilization, a helpless, pink animal with no radio, no supplies, and no weapons—but with a dedicated determination to survive until his rescuers came, and to tell of what he had seen. A human being who had looked on the Kilroys and lived. . . .

Chapter Sixteen

*It never ceases to amaze me that woman's
attraction for man is always the same attraction.*
CHARLES SALLOWS

Looking through the open glass doors that led onto
the balcony, Tom Bruce could see the impossibly
large orange moon trailing its path of light over the
calm, blue-black sea. The air of the room was warm
and heavy with that sweet yet curiously animal perfume which he knew would always be associated in
his memory with this night. He raised himself on one
elbow and looked across the enormous round bed that
Elsa Prince called her "playground."

She lay in feline relaxation, her naked oiled body
glistening like ebony against the paleness of the
sheets. He had assumed that she was sleeping, but he
saw now that he was wrong. Her eyes, large and
glowing, with a strange fluorescence, were watching
him.

"Welcome back," she said in her throaty, mocking
purr. "I was beginning to think you'd pooped out."

"Just getting my breath," he said.

"And maybe your second wind?"

"Or fourth. . .or is it fifth?"

"Who's counting?" she said, moving toward him.

He lay quite still as she placed one hand on his chest and began to slide it gently downwards. He could already feel his passion mounting again. He had known women—many women, of all shapes, sizes and inclinations—but never one quite like Elsa. Sex with her was a new kind of experience, taking him beyond the known borderlines of sensation and pleasure into a new country of dangerous, savage delights. She was a succubus, a vampire, taking all in the fire of her sensuality and transmuting it to her own purposes. He sensed this ravenous greed in her, and yet at the same time the skill with which she transmitted the echo of that same pleasure back to him made him content.

Earlier he had suffered his qualms of conscience, the reminders that this was the wife of Robert Prince, his friend. But as the night wore on, any kind of shame was the first casualty. His misgivings had retreated further and further into the background, helped to do so by the certain knowledge that these things she was doing with him she had done with others, many times. . . He was not responsible for the cuckolding. The horns must have been hung on Robert Prince long ago by this woman for whom no one man could ever hope to provide permanent satisfaction. He wondered if Bob knew and was perhaps content to share what he could not possess entirely. How would he himself act in the same situation? A man had his pride, but a woman like this could get in your blood, perhaps conditioning a special kind of hunger that only she could satisfy. It would be like being hooked on a drug—and probably equally destructive.

He would never allow her to do that to him. But for tonight, just for tonight, he would taste all the dangerous fruit she offered. He grabbed for her, intent on asserting his masculine role, but her smooth flesh slipped from under his fingers as the top half of her body moved upright. She looked down at him, a black silhouette with glowing eyes.

"Lie still!" she commanded. "This time I'll show you some *real* action."

The sound was immediately familiar, an insistent, penetrating *beep. . .beep. . .beep. . .beep. .* going on and on, nagging, demanding his attention unconditionally. Habit and discipline were so deeply ingrained that he did the only thing possible for him. Sliding from beneath her at the very moment of penetration, he bounded off the bed and fumbled in the breast pocket of his civilian casual jacket.

The beeping stopped as he pressed the button on his personal communicator and said: "Commander Bruce here—yes?"

"Triple A Emergency orders just received. *Vee Twelve* to lift off for Orphelin system at earliest." The voice was that of Helen Lindstrom, and even through the tiny speaker of the communicator he felt that he could detect the cold disapproval of her tone.

"Right! How do I get back?" he snapped.

"Pursuit copter is on its way from Tenerife—ETA five minutes from now."

"Good! I'll be waiting," he said. "Anything else?"

"Make a direct scrambled call to President Fong immediately on your return."

"Will do. Bruce—out." He thrust the communicator back into the jacket pocket, then turned to find himself facing Elsa's glowing eyes.

She flung herself at him, using nails, teeth, and all the surprising strength of her small body to cleave him to her.

"You kept me waiting, you bastard!" She moaned and sobbed, writhing against him. "Come on! Now! Now!"

"No, Elsa," he said firmly, grasping hold of her shoulders and pushing her away from him. "You heard the communicator. That copter will be here soon and I don't want to keep it waiting."

"The hell with that!" she screamed. "What difference is a few minutes going to make? We've got some unfinished business, remember?"

"I'm sorry," he said, "but that's the way it has to be. Now, will you let me put my clothes on?"

She tore herself from his grasp and backed away, snarling and spitting like a wildcat. "That Scandinavian cow Lindstrom! This was her idea, wasn't it? Anything to stop her darling commander from getting himself laid by someone else."

"Now you know that is complete nonsense," he said, slipping into his trousers. "She would hardly be likely to invent a Triple A Emergency just to get me out of your bed—even if she gave a damn, which I seriously doubt." He reached across to the light-switch. The rosy, concealed lighting of the ceiling flicked on.

Elsa stood there, her shining naked body vibrating with tension, the image of her father suddenly appearing, ugly and vulpine, in her face.

"You bastard! You bloody tin-soldier, Corps-loving bastard! Who needs you? You couldn't fuck your way out of a paper bag! Get the hell out of my bedroom!"

Chapter Seventeen

*Conscience is a cur that will let you get past
it but that you cannot keep from barking.*

ANON

"Sorry to break in on your little vacation, Bruce," said Henry Fong. "But we had a report in from Excelsior a couple of hours ago that their colony on Orphelin Three has been off the air since the day before yesterday."

"And they only just decided to tell us?" Bruce said, staring at the smooth, unruffled features of the President. "Don't they know the drill?"

"Niebohr made some excuse about hanging on in the hope that the hiatus was merely due to a technical fault. He's pretty involved with the Orphelin thing, and you know he doesn't like to call in the Corps if he can possibly avoid it."

"On principle, or for some particular reason in this case?" Bruce said.

"Possibly both," Fong replied unhelpfully. "How long will it take you to get there?"

Bruce shrugged. "A hundred and forty-five hours, more or less."

"Make it a hundred and forty," Fong said. "We may have another Kepler III type incident on our hands."

"You suspect Kilroy activity?"

"It is always a possibility," Fong said. "That's why I'm sending you and *Vee Twelve*. You have the experience."

"And the record of always arriving too late," said Bruce with a touch of bitterness. "If this is a Kilroy operation they'll be away to hell and gone by now— three, four days. . . They don't usually sit around to gloat, you know."

"I'm well aware of that," Fong said blandly. "But there may be survivors, and there's always a chance you might learn something."

"Like just how impotent we are? Mr. President, get me that Warp Drive and I'll really deliver you some facts—maybe even a bunch of Kilroy pelts."

"We're working on it," said Fong.

"And if I do find that the whole thing is a simple communications failure?"

"Then we shall all be truly thankful," Fong said. "But whatever you find, Commander Bruce, you will report directly to me. Is that understood?"

"Yes, Mr. President."

"Then the blessing of the Supreme Being be with you, Commander. . .and keep your powder dry."

Fong's image faded, and Bruce turned from the blank screen to Helen Lindstrom, who had been standing nearby during the conversation.

"If I wasn't sure that it was impossible, I'd guess that Fong knows more about this operation than he's telling," he said.

"Henry Fong *always* knows more than he's telling,"

she said, her blue eyes scrutinizing him critically. "I'd get Maseba to fix me some shots, if I were you. You look like hell."

"And you're out of line, Commander," snapped Bruce. "What's the ready situation?"

"Liftoff in. . ." she glanced at the wall clock, ". . .eight minutes, fifty seconds from now."

"Very good, Commander. You take it from the bridge. I'll join you in a couple of minutes."

"Yessir," said Lindstrom, turning to leave. She paused in the doorway, looking back at him, a half-smile on her handsome features. "I still say you look like hell. I think maybe I saved your life with that call. You're getting kind of old for marathon shagging."

"OUT!" growled Bruce.

The scout from *Venturer Twelve* leaned as hard on its antigravs as was permissible. Lieutenant (M) Leela De Witt was with Lindstrom as they descended in a shallow spiral. Lindstrom watched the dire, interminable stretches of ruin below them; De Witt was concerned with the radiation hazards coming from the horrid black scab that once had been a happy, prosperous planet.

Lindstrom did not resent the fact that she had been sent down, rather than a man, to head the reconnaissance team. In the Corps, there were only officers; on duty, there was no difference. But she knew that the sense of outrage she felt came from her being a woman; she resented the waste of life.

"Are we going to get down safely?" she asked.

"If we don't stay on surface more than one hour Earth, and if everyone's suit is one hundred percent, and if no one does anything stupid, yes."

Lindstrom began to zip up the double closures of the rough-textured a/r suit. "It can get through this?"

"I'm not certain, so I'm on the safe side. If I did anything else, George Maseba would carve me up for the spare-parts." When she smiled, her fragile Hindu beauty showed cheerfully.

"All personnel zip and check suits," Lindstrom ordered. She peered down at the world whose surface was like a black, evil ghost of its former self. "P.O. Ashnagabi, put us down on the big oval—the sports ground."

"Yes, ma'am."

At five meters, the charred dust stirred under the antigravs' pressure. Then they touched down. Lindstrom gave her final orders. "Normal use of lock. Don't hurry. You all have your personal coms, and a map. Check needlers; you may have to kill some mad wreck who survived. Leading Crewman Griffiths, switch on each a/g lift separately before you push it outboard. If anyone is fool enough to stand in front of the lift slot, I'll fine him a month's pay, if he lives. Any questions?"

Her face was impassive, but she thought: *What am I trying to do? Copy Tom Bruce?*

No one gave any answers.

Bruce's personal conviction was that the Kilroys were long gone. Nevertheless, the ship, orbiting Orphelin III, was and remained at full battle alert. Whatever the fire-power ratio was with that of the enemy, he could not take chances, and therefore he had avoided taking the ship down to surface, where she would be a sitting duck for any potential enemy. Thus, he was forced to wait, scowling at his main screen and speculating on the carbonized destruction that seemed to obliterate the entire continental mass and sully the planet's predominantly blue image.

"Well?" he demanded when Lindstrom's face at last appeared on the screen.

She gazed at him for a moment, her features stiff, as if frozen with the horror of what she had seen. "It's bad," she said at last. The words seemed to issue unwilling from her mouth. "We landed on the outskirts of what used to be Josiahtown. There's nothing left standing, just a flattened plain of charred rubble. I've never seen anything like it."

"Survivors?" barked Bruce.

"Not a chance," Lindstrom said. "If anybody had lived through the initial blast, the radioactivity would have gotten them by now. I've sent parties out to search the surface, but even wearing heavy-duty suits they won't be able to do more than a fifty-minute tour. In any case, I'm pretty sure that it's hopeless." Her eyes stared at him, pleading for some comfort. "Over two hundred and fifty thousand people lived here, Tom. Two hundred thousand—"

"And the other towns?" Bruce pursued with deliberate directness, knowing that it would be unwise to allow her to dwell on her present train of thought. Helen was a good—a first class—officer, but there were times when her female sensitivity could be a disadvantage.

"The copters are on their way now, to check, but from what we saw on the way down I don't think the outlook for them will be any better. It looks like a typical Kilroy mass-extermination job."

Bruce nodded. "What about the islands?"

"I'm going to take a look at them as soon as we've done a complete check of the continental land mass," Lindstrom said. "According to briefing, this is where the people were, so if there are any survivors it's essential that we lose no time in getting to them. Do you agree?"

"Yes, of course," Bruce said. "Rescue of survivors must have top priority, although I don't suppose the poor devils will be able to tell us a great deal. They'll probably have less idea than we have already of just what hit them."

She was looking at him again, the shocked rigidity creeping back into her features. "Tom, why would they do it? The Kilroys, I mean—"

"For God's sake, woman! Pull yourself together!" snapped Bruce. "How can we possibly make any sense in guessing their reasons? Maybe Orphelin Three was the site of another one of their experiments that went wrong—like Kepler and those things on Minos IV. Or maybe they just had some new weapon they wanted to test. Forget about that kind of conjecture. Your job is to gather all the available information."

"Yes, sir," she said, and he was pleased to see the animation of anger in her features. That way she would work better and efficiently, with less time for dangerous introspection.

"Carry on, Commander Lindstrom!" he ordered, breaking the connection.

Now it was a return to the waiting game. There was absolutely nothing he could do until Helen's mission was completed. Then he would be able to send his preliminary report to Fong back on Earth and request further orders, the nature of which he could already guess. What else could they be but instructions to return to base? There was nothing he could do here in the Orphelin system—the Kilroys had already moved on, about their unguessable business. He rose from his chair and began to walk away, but before he had reached the door the sudden clangor of the ship's alarm system burst into life.

The banshee howling of the sirens damped down almost immediately, to be superseded by the urgent voice of Lieutenant Maranne, the radar officer in charge of detection units.

"UFO approaching at estimated speed three-quarters light, bearing 360, coordinates 67C by 28D.

"Hear this! Hear this! UFO approaching at bearing 195, coordinates 67C by 28D—estimated speed point O Seven Light. Alert all gunnery and missile systems! Hear this! Hear this! UFO approaching at bearing. . ."

Bruce hurried along the corridor in the direction of Operations Control at a run, muttering a prayer that this time at least he might get a chance to strike back at the will-o-the-wisp enemy.

The air in Operations Control seemed to crackle with tension as all the duty personnel sat unnaturally silent at their posts. Maranne, a coffee-skinned beauty with short-cropped black hair close to her head like a furry cap, was at her station on the main dais, overlooking the rest of the setup. Bruce hurried up to join her.

"What have you got?" he demanded.

She pointed down into the spherical simulator with a light-pencil, indicating the slow-moving, bright red blip.

"For the moment he's just Charlie Nobody," she said tersely. "We're still waiting for a reply to our identification request."

Bruce looked across at the main information display. "And your Charlie will be well in range in three and a half minutes." He dropped into the chair beside her and thumbed a button. The face of Lee Hoon

Hock, chief gunnery officer, appeared in one of his monitor screens.

"Sir?"

"Lee, I want you to launch a clutch of Engelschafts—now!"

"You've identified the UFO as alien?"

"No—nothing through yet."

"But, sir—"

Bruce's face darkened. "Lieutenant, I am not going to miss this opportunity; shoot!"

"Yes, sir." Lee's startled face disappeared from the screen to reappear again less than thirty seconds later. "Missiles launched, sir."

Bruce grunted an acknowledgment and swung his chair to look down into the simulator. A bright green line, which soon separated into six individual threads, began to crawl out from the image of V 12, heading in the direction of the UFO.

"Acknowledgment coming in now," said Maranne's urgent voice at his elbow.

He turned his chair and sat waiting impatiently through the brief time-lag while the ship's communications computor re-recorded the message and eliminated the Doppler distortion.

All heads in the room turned, attention riveted, as the main screen burst into life to reveal the head and shoulders of a man in the blue uniform of a merchant spacer.

"Excelsior Corporation freighter *Medusa*, ex-Earth, Fleet Director Robert Prince commanding. Repeat, identification: Excelsior Corporation freighter. . ."

"Blast!" growled Bruce, punching his console again.

The face of Lee appeared.

"Destruct missiles!" ordered Bruce.

"Yes, sir."

The right-hand monitor screen flared into brief and brilliant light as three million credits' worth of missiles exploded in empty space.

"Sound stand-down," Bruce said to Maranne. "And take *Medusa* off the main screen. I'll talk to them direct."

The main screen went blank, and the face of the *Medusa* operator appeared on Bruce's central monitor.

"Commander Bruce, Corps ship *Venturer Twelve* here—get me Commander Prince."

"Tom, you bellicose bastard! You nearly blew my arse off!" said Prince a moment later. "What's going on?"

"Kilroy strike on Orphelin Three," Bruce said tersely.

"Bad?"

"Prelim reports indicate the entire colony wiped out."

"My God!" exclaimed Prince, his thinly handsome face reflecting his consternation. "Are you sure?"

"Lindstrom's still down there searching," Bruce said, "but I can't give you much hope. Everything on the main land mass is flattened, for sure."

"Is there anything I can do?"

"Better leave it to Lindstrom, for the time being at least—she's got the equipment to cope."

"Poppa Niebohr's going to blow his skull over this one," Prince said. "Orphelin Three was his special baby. He had a man named MacGuinness doing a thorough fishery survey. What about the islands, by the way?"

Bruce shrugged. "As far as we can see from here they're untouched. But that doesn't help a lot, does it? All the population was on the main continent."

"Well, yes," said Prince. "But MacGuinness and whoever he has with him might still be down there among the islands, if the destruction didn't reach that far."

"I'll have Lindstrom make a thorough check when she's finished on Tantaron," Bruce said. "Now how about you? What are you doing around Orphelin?"

"Special assignment from Poppa," Prince said. "I dropped off a team of geologists and engineers at Orphelin Four on the way out and then headed for Balomain. When I heard the all-channels emergency call I decided to turn back."

"In that case you must have had a very close call," Bruce said. "The alien attack took place only a few hours after you left the Orphelin system. About this team of yours—have you contacted them yet?"

"No. With your permission I'd like to carry on over to Four and pick them up."

"Of course," said Bruce. "They may be able to give us some lead on the Kilroys."

Prince nodded. "I doubt it, but I'll come over and match orbits with you once we've got them safely aboard. Have you reported back to Earth yet?"

"No. I'm waiting for Lindstrom's full report before doing that," said Bruce, then added, "I'd appreciate it if you didn't send anything either, for the time being. We've got to get our facts right on this thing."

"Naturally," said Prince. "See you in a few hours' time. . . By the way, how was Elsa when you left?"

Bruce had a sudden vision of dark, oiled limbs and a once-attractive face distorted by hate. "Elsa. . . ? Oh, she was fine. See you." He switched off abruptly, turning away from the screen in a spasm of self-disgust. That whoring bitch! How could he ever have allowed her to lure him into betraying a straight, honest guy like Prince? He suddenly felt dirty.

"I'll be in my cabin when Lindstrom calls," he said to Maranne as he rose to his feet. "Put her through to me there, will you?"

"Yes, sir," she said. He hurried out of Operations Control, aware of her watching, curious eyes.

Chapter Eighteen

Here, we work close together or perish
On new lands a lifetime from home;
All other men's skills we must cherish,
All other men's hearts are our own.
        Thunder of Stars: IVAN KAVANIN

The tangle-haired, filthy, scarecrow figure that had once been known as Angus MacGuinness squatted in the shaded hollow concentrating all that remained of his eroded intelligence on the task before him. Naked, his body covered with festering sores and wracked by fever, he murmured obscenities like some mysterious incantation as he twirled the pointed piece of hard wood in the socket for what seemed like the millionth time.

MacGuinness had found out the hard way that even on a paradise planet life can be tough and brutish without the material benefits of civilization. The nights that once seemed so invigorating with their wine-like sea breezes were now cold, damp eternities of blackness filled with shivering fear; the days, with a pitiless sun that burned into his skin and scratched mercilessly at his streaming, red-rimmed eyes, were little better. Then there were the insects, which fed happily on exposed flesh no longer protected by clothing or repellent ointments, some of them depositing their eggs beneath the surface of the skin to create yet more festering sores on the already rotting hide. For food there had been berries and wild fruits—an error of choice had almost killed him on the second day, when he had lain for almost twenty-four hours writhing and retching while all the demons of hell seemed to be tearing at the inside of his gut—and, when he needed variety, he forced himself to overcome his instinctive nausea and eat a species of fat white grub that had a sweet/salty taste.

Combined with his will to live, he felt that this diet might well serve to sustain him until some form of rescue appeared, if only he could have some kind of warmth. That simplest-seeming, most taken-for-granted aspect of human comfort, a fire, loomed enormous and desirable in his mind, filling his every waking thought. All his learning and intelligence were suddenly valueless in the face of this basic problem, and he found added frustration in the knowledge that savages since time began had been capable of creating this miracle which had eluded him for three whole days.

Taking the stick once more between his bony, cold-stiffened palms, he twirled it in a grim frenzy of determination. The tiniest wisp of grey smoke rose and dissipated quickly into the cool air. He twirled the stick again, a cracked giggle of triumph dribbling from his lips.

More smoke this time, faltering at first, then pouring upwards in a nostril-clogging, eye-irritating stream as he bent down and cupped the tuft of dried grass between his two hands, breathing on it gently, fearfully. . .

The flicker of flame grew stronger. He piled on another handful of grass with his right hand, scarcely heeding the fact that the skin of his left was burning. . . Then a few dry twigs, carefully, gently. . . and there it was, at last, a real fire.

He straightened up with a whoop of triumph, waving his fist in the direction of the setting sun. He was sure now that he *would* survive another night—that he would have some warmth—and tomorrow rescue must surely come.

He hardly noticed the first oily drops of rain—the skin of his body was becoming hardened to pain and to other stimuli in consequence. But soon the drops became a torrent.

Conscious of the danger to his newly kindled fire, he bent over it, trying to shield it from the deluge. The smell of burning hair mingled with the smoke for a few brief seconds, and then the fire sizzled and died under the impact of the water pouring over his back and shoulders.

With a howl of sheer despair Angus MacGuinness slumped over the damp, dead ashes of his fire. As the delirium closed in on his mind his last sane thought was the recognition that, in addition to the rest of his troubles, it was quite possible that the rain would be radioactive. . . .

Lindstrom's face was tired but alert, and Bruce was pleased to see that her eyes had lost their haunted look. Even a sensitive mind such as hers could become habituated to horror with the help of time and concentration on the task at hand.

"It seems that our first estimate about the unlikelihood of survivors was correct," she said. "There's no doubt now that the entire population of the Tantaron continent has been destroyed. My copters and a/g lift men have completed their search pattern without detecting the slightest sign of life."

Bruce nodded. "A typically thorough Kilroy extermination job."

"Well yes, but. . ."

"But what?" Bruce was immediately alert.

"I think it's a bit early in our experience of them to talk about a typical Kilroy attack, don't you?"

"What are you getting at?" Bruce demanded impatiently.

"Well, it was your remark about their having some new weapon they wanted to test that started me off," Helen said, frowning. "You remember that ray of theirs that burned Kepler III to slag?"

"I'm not likely to forget it."

"As an extermination instrument, wouldn't you say that was about as efficient as you can get?"

"So?"

"It's just that our survey down here makes it pretty clear that the destruction was caused by either a very powerful multiple-warhead missile or a number of individual missiles," said Helen. "Now it seems to me that this constitutes a retrograde step in weaponry rather than an advance. I mean, why bother with old-fashioned nuclear bombs when you can stand off from a planet maybe ten million miles and do what they did to Kepler III?"

"Maybe they wanted to be more selective this time," suggested Bruce.

"Leaving the islands untouched, you mean? Could be," admitted Lindstrom. "My boys are on their way down there now; maybe they'll find some clue. . .

Even so, I can't help feeling there's something strange about their using missiles—and not particularly efficient ones at that, it seems. One of the copters working along the western coastline reported what seems to be an unexploded bomb about five kilometers out in the ocean."

Bruce shot bolt upright in his seat. "For God's sake, woman! Do you realize what you're saying? For the first time ever we have a chance of getting our hands on a piece of Kilroy weaponry."

"A perfectly ordinary nuclear bomb—"

"That's not the point," said Bruce angrily. "This is a Kilroy-manufactured bomb. Examination of it is sure to tell our experts at least something about their technology."

"Maybe. . . But it's standing about twenty fathoms deep, according to the report."

"I don't care if it's a hundred fathoms. I want that missile, so get working on it!" barked Bruce.

Lindstrom winced visibly. "Yes, sir. Any other instructions?"

"Yes. Tell your people searching the islands to look out for a man named MacGuinness. Robert Prince tells me that he is down there doing a fishery survey for Niebohr."

"Prince? When did you talk to him?"

"He arrived in the Orphelin system a couple of hours ago, commanding an Excelsior freighter."

"Well I'll be damned!" exclaimed Lindstrom. "Small universe, isn't it? You two must have a lot to talk about, one way or another."

"Very funny!" snapped Bruce. "You just keep that kind of smart-ass talk to yourself and get on with the job of fishing for that missile—understood?"

"Loud and clear, sir," Lindstrom's face faded from

the screen, but it seemed to Bruce that her curious grin lingered like that of Alice's Cheshire Cat.

Lieutenant (M) Leela De Witt's brown face was grave as she looked down at the pathetic, naked wreck of a human being that lay unconscious on the stretcher.

"Will he live?" asked Helen Lindstrom.

"I'm not about to commit myself on a question like that at this stage," De Witt said. "At first glance I'd say he's suffering from exposure, some kind of unidentified fever, burns, and a whole heap of minor infections and abrasions. When we really get down to it, there may be a number of other items that need attention."

Lindstrom nodded. "He's sure taken some punishment, even I can see that. I wonder if he's that biologist Bruce mentioned?"

"Whoever he is, I doubt if his own mother would know him right now," De Witt said. "How soon can we get him back up to *Vee Twelve?*"

"You can't treat him here?"

She shrugged. "I can give him a few shots and some plasma, but if I'm to do a really good job I need to have him in the sick bay."

"It's urgent?"

"One way or another, this poor guy's had about as much as he can take," said De Witt. "No single one of the things he has wrong with him is likely to kill him immediately—but the combination. . ."

Helen Lindstrom gnawed at her bottom lip. "Tom Bruce will probably have the hide off me for leaving the planet's surface before they've fished that missile up."

"If he does, tell him I overrode you," Do Witt said.

"Apart from any consideration of a humanitarian nature, this poor sod looks like he's the only survivor out of the entire planetary population. I'd say that makes him a pretty important guy, wouldn't you?"

Lindstrom smiled briefly. "You just got yourself a deal, Leela. That missile can wait until I've done the return trip."

Tom Bruce and Helen Lindstrom stood outside the intensive care unit looking through the transparent wall as Surgeon Commander George Maseba and Leela de Witt worked over the scarecrow body of Angus MacGuinness.

"If he makes it, he'll be about the luckiest guy in the universe," said Helen.

Tom Bruce nodded. "Pity he isn't going to be able to tell us anything much about the attack. How are your people coming along with that unexploded missile, by the way?"

"They're working on it," Helen said. "But they're having to be pretty careful. It seems that the casing is cracked and the leakage of radioactivity is way up."

"That's hardly surprising under the circumstances," Bruce said. He wheeled to face a breathless petty officer who had just sprinted up behind them. "Yes?"

"Sir, Lieutenant Maranne reports that Excelsior Corporation freighter *Medusa* has broken orbit and is heading out of the Orphelin system at maximum acceleration."

"The hell she is!" exclaimed Bruce. He began to hurry in the direction of the Operations Room via the main lift.

"What's your pal Prince playing at now?" asked Helen, who was close beside him.

"Damned if I know!" Bruce said angrily. "I told

him to match orbits with us as soon as he'd picked up those geologists from Orphelin Four, and it's not like Prince to disobey a direct order."

"He's not Corps any more, remember?"

"Maybe so, but he realizes that somebody has to be in charge in a situation of this kind," said Bruce as they entered Operations.

Lieutenant Maranne looked up as they approached. "I thought you'd want to know immediately, sir," she said.

"You're damned right I do," said Bruce. "Get *Medusa* right away!"

"I've been trying for the last three minutes, sir," explained Maranne. "They just don't answer."

"Dammit!" exclaimed Bruce angrily. "Ex-Corpsman or not, I'll see that Prince doesn't get even a flycar license after this."

"There may be some logical explanation," suggested Lindstrom.

"If there is, it had better be a good one," said Bruce. "Direct disobedience of orders in an emergency situation of this nature—I could throw the book at him and then some."

"Lieutenant Lee calling from Orphelin Three for you, ma'am," Maranne said to Helen, interrupting Bruce's tirade.

"Put him on this monitor," Helen said.

The dark-haired, earnest face of young Lee Hoon Hock appeared on the screen. He seemed to be having some trouble finding his words, and there was a great deal more of the whites of his eyes showing than usual.

"Yes, Lee—what is it? Have you managed to get the missile up?" asked Helen.

Lee swallowed. "Yes, ma'am. I. . .I think you'd better come down here right away."

"Why? What is it, Lee? Something gone wrong?" asked Lindstrom.

"Ma'am, I just don't know how to explain. . ." Lee said unhappily.

Chapter Nineteen

History can only be described as "bunk" when the history makers of today refuse to see their own image in the blunders of the history makers of the past.

The Wit and Wisdom of Henry Fong (p. 573)

Henry Fong was standing by the window. He turned as Elkan Niebohr entered the room, and the visitor found himself shocked by the President's appearance. The small body seemed to have shrunk, so that the normally neat, plain high-necked jacket appeared baggy and shapeless. Moving closer, he became aware that the deceptively smooth, youthful-appearing face seemed suddenly aged and haggard.

"Mr. President, I came immediately when I received your call," he said, taking the small bony hand in his own large paw.

Fong nodded. "Please sit down," he said, lowering himself tiredly into an armchair. He waited until Niebohr had done the same before continuing. "I received a preliminary report from Commander Bruce just over an hour ago."

Niebohr started forward in his seat.

"I'm afraid the news is grave," said the President, his parchment-yellow face solemn. "The entire Orphelin Three colony has been destroyed and the continent of Tantaron is a charred, radioactive ruin that will remain incapable of supporting life for many years."

In the thirty-second silence, Niebohr stared woodenly.

"There are no survivors?" he asked.

"None at all. The destruction is complete and utter."

"Five million people—God!" Elkan Niebohr slumped forward in his chair, burying his face in his hands.

"I know that it must be a terrible blow for you to bear, Elkan," said the President's gentle, high-pitched voice. "Your personal involvement with the Orphelin Three colony is well known."

Niebohr straightened up and looked directly into the President's dark, sympathetic eyes. "Every one of those people was like my own flesh and blood," he said. "They named their cities, their children after me. . . And now it's all gone. Orphelin was more than a business operation to me; its success, the lives of all those happy, healthy people—the whole thing had come to have a very special meaning."

"I understand only too well, Elkan," said the President. "But we must learn to accept such misfortune as part of the Supreme Being's inscrutable plan."

Niebohr's hawk features hardened. "I'm afraid I don't have that consolation. If this Supreme Being of yours really exists, then that implies that he is also the creator of these fiends, these Kilroy creatures who prey upon our colonies and destroy our innocent people." Niebohr seemed deeply shaken.

"As he is also the creator of the savage beast and the infinitely small virus—both of which live through the destruction of others," Fong said blandly. "It is not given to us to understand such mysteries."

"Surely that's not all you have to offer?" Niebohr stared at this tiny, aging man with a growing contempt. At times like this it seemed to him that Henry Fong was more suited to the secluded life of a Buddhist monk than to the task of guiding the destiny of mankind's hundred and fifty inhabited worlds. To greet a situation like this with mouthings about the workings of the Supreme Being was to abdicate from responsibility.

"My dear Elkan—whatever we do or say, nothing can alter the grim reality of the destruction of the Orphelin Three colony."

"Minos. . .Kepler. . .Orphelin," Niebohr intoned the list bitterly. "And next? Another of the colonies —or Earth itself? How much longer must we go on waiting to be destroyed like a flock of sheep?"

"I am aware of the gravity of the situation," said Fong. "We have discussed it on other occasions."

"But still nothing is *done!*" said Niebohr, his voice deep with anger. "Time after time the Corps appears on the scene too late to do anything but survey the damage."

"As you know, we are hoping that the Warp Drive may change that situation," said Fong.

"I'm beginning to doubt that," Niebohr said. "Even with such a drive, the Corps will be able to do little more than sit around and wait for news of the next strike. The time lag may be shortened—but the chances are that they will still be too late to take any effective action. It seems to me that it is long past time that the people of United Earth were made aware of the true facts of the situation. They must be told about the destruction of Orphelin Three in the fullest detail—and they must be made fully aware of the manner in which their protection is being neglected. They have a right to the facts, and I shall make it my business to tell them."

"My dear Elkan, I can fully understand the reasons for your indignation," Fong said gently. "But I'm afraid I cannot allow you to follow such an ill-considered and alarmist course of action."

"But that is deliberate suppression," objected Niebohr. "The people have a right to know these things."

"While I admire your democratic principles, I'm afraid I have no intention of changing my decision in this matter," Fong said. "If I am proved wrong in the long run, then history will be my judge—but for the time being I must do what I consider the best thing."

"In that case, I suppose there is nothing more to be said," growled Niebohr. He began to rise to his feet.

"Just a moment, Elkan," Fong said quietly. "There is one other small matter."

Niebohr settled back warily in his seat, his eyes watching Fong alertly. "Yes?"

"Your son-in-law, Robert Prince—what was the purpose of his visit to the Orphelin system?"

"He paused there on his way to Balomain to drop off a party of geologists and engineers on Orphelin Four," said Niebohr. "We are in the process of investigating both planets in the hope that one of them will provide a suitable base for the activities of Koninburger."

"Yes, I see," Fong said, nodding. "I had guessed

that the journey was connected with something of that nature. However, it seems that on hearing the emergency warning about Orphelin Three he immediately turned back from his projected journey and appeared in the Orphelin system shortly after the arrival of *Venturer Twelve.*"

"Considering the fact that he is commanding a standard-type freighter, I would think it a rather damning judgment on Corps efficiency that he was able to do so," Niebohr said.

"You are of course entitled to take that view," Fong replied. "But there is also the point to be borne in mind that he happened to be, through some quirk of chance, the nearest ship to the Orphelin system at the time of the tragedy. However, that is unimportant. What is a great deal more serious is the fact that, having reported his presence to *Venturer Twelve* in accordance with Emergency Procedure—which, as you know, makes the acceptance of orders from the Corps officer in charge obligatory upon any merchant ship in the vicinity—he then saw fit to leave the Orphelin system in direct contravention of Bruce's orders."

Niebohr frowned. "He no doubt had a good reason for doing so."

"Possibly. . ." Fong said thoughtfully. "At any rate, he will have ample opportunity to explain to the tribunal."

"Tribunal! What the devil are you talking about?"

"Merely the fact that Bruce has filed preliminary charges against Robert Prince for having disobeyed orders in a Triple A Emergency situation."

"Bruce! That stiff-necked martinet!" exclaimed Niebohr angrily. "He's only doing this out of personal spite."

"Really? Now that's interesting," Fong said. "I was under the impression that he and Prince were long-standing friends, but perhaps you know something more on the subject?"

"I know nothing, except the fact that Bruce would do anything to get at me in any way possible—whether through Robert Prince or anyone else."

Henry Fong regarded his visitor, his head slightly to one side. "Well, of course, if you would like to file a counter-charge along those lines, I'm sure the tribunal would be pleased to hear your evidence—but even so I doubt that it would entirely nullify the seriousness of Prince's situation. You see, as an ex-Corpsman himself, he must be fully aware of the manner in which he has violated Regulations."

"Where is *Medusa* now?" asked Niebohr.

Fong spread his bony hands, palms uppermost. "As far as we know she is on her way back to Earth. Prince will be arrested as soon as he lands, of course." He rose to his feet and stood for a moment looking down at his guest. His face had once more resumed its egg-like inscrutability. "And now I must ask you to excuse me. There are several urgent matters pressing. In the meantime, please give my sincere regards to your charming daughter."

Elkan Niebohr left the Presidential presence aware of a vague, uncomfortable feeling at the back of his mind that when Henry Fong spoke of the mysterious workings of the Supreme Being, he was in some oblique manner referring to the complicated web of his own maneuvers. The idea that it was possible he was being used was not one which Elkan Niebohr could accept with complacency.

Chapter Twenty

*Nature has given women so much power that
the law has very wisely given them little.*
SAMUEL JOHNSON

She came in through the doorway of his private study wearing a pants suit of a filmy material that looked like spun gold. Her hair was upswept in an elaborately lacquered style, emphasizing the strong beauty of her features.

"Tell me how I look, Poppa," she said, grinning at him.

"You know darned well how you look," he said with a fond chuckle. "But don't you think you might have put some underwear on beneath that thing?"

"And spoil the effect?"

"Any woman who walks around looking like that is asking to be either fucked or arrested."

"I don't want to go to jail, Poppa," she said, moving across the room and perching herself on the corner of his desk like some golden bird. "When do I get my Prince Charming back?"

"I thought you'd made other arrangements," he said, looking up at her with some surprise.

156

"Like that bastard Bruce? Don't remind me! Next time I'll fix him."

"Hell hath no fury. . . ?"

"Aw Christ, Poppa, do you have to be so angular?" she said grimacing. "I don't give a damn about him really—but he left me wanting, and that's not the way I operate."

"You'll have another score to settle with him when he gets back," said Niebohr. "He's filed charges against Robert for disobeying orders in an emergency situation and leaving the Orphelin system without his permission. The President himself told me a couple of hours ago."

"The bastard!" she repeated. "And I thought he and Robert were supposed to be such old chums."

"They were, but that doesn't count for much with a Corps-lover like Bruce. He's the kind who goes by the book whoever is involved."

"And if these charges stick—what then?"

"A big fine, and maybe the loss of his master's certificate for a year or two," Niebohr said. "We can handle it. But that kind of thing doesn't look good on the man I've named as my successor."

"You'll fix it, Poppa—you always do," she said. "Take this Orphelin deal, for instance."

Niebohr stiffened. "We don't talk about that, not even between ourselves," he said.

She grinned down at him like a sensual cat-creature. "What's the matter—you afraid dear old Henry Fong might have slipped a few bugs in? Relax, Poppa, the whole thing's over now. *The Kilroys Strike Again*— that's the name of the comedy, isn't it?"

"I can't see anything funny in the death of five million peoople," Niebohr said frowning.

"Five, six million—what difference does it make?

At that distance they're just statistics, and you know it," Elsa said. "Don't try to be pious with me, Poppa —if you're really grieving over anything, it's the sixty million credits a year you're going to lose in imports from Orphelin Three."

He looked up at her, aware of a curious mixture of disapproval and admiration in his mind. Those five million people might well be statistics to Elsa, but for him there were certain faces he remembered —Charles Cromlech, the Excelsior administrator on Orphelin Three, his wife, a striking blonde with brown eyes, and their three small daughters. . . He thrust the train of thought aside impatiently. There was no point in looking back. Nothing could be undone. Orphelin Three had shown a profit for over twenty years —that was on the credit side. He had no illusions about the permanency of the writing off—there would be no attempt made to resettle the planet during his lifetime. But while it remained uninhabited there would be no twenty-five-year inspection by the Colonization Commission experts, and no question of the secret uncovered by MacGuinness being exposed again.

"What the hell was Bob doing in the Orphelin system anyway?" Elsa's voice broke in on his thoughts. "I thought he was supposed to go on to Balomain after dropping off Kurt Wernher and his team?"

"He was—but when he heard the Emergency signal about Orphelin, he turned back."

She shook her head from side to side, smiling quietly. "Good old Bob. . .I can just picture him riding to the rescue like a knight in shining amor. I know you think he's a pompous fool, but he really is— what was that old word?—chivalrous? When he talks in his stiff-upper-lip way about things like Honesty and Truth you begin to wonder if maybe they might not exist after all."

Was she serious? He looked up at her, scrutinizing the beautiful mystery of her face, and found himself reminded yet again that, although she was his own flesh and the dearest human being in the universe to him, she remained an enigma.

"You're laughing at me, Poppa," she accused.

"No, never that, baby," he said. "Never that."

She dropped from her perch on the desk and moved restlessly about the room.

"I've been wondering about Kurt Wernher," she said thoughtfully. "Do you think that after this we shall be able to go on trusting him?"

"Why shouldn't we?"

"He's ambitious, Poppa, and he knows a great deal. . ."

"Knowledge is power, you mean?"

"He could ruin you, if he wanted to."

"And himself at the same time," Niebohr pointed out. "That is not something Kurt Wernher would undertake lightly. He's good—the best there is in his own specialty."

"There are other hatchet men."

"But few of them with his intelligence," said Niebohr.

"But he's dangerous, make no mistake about that, Poppa," Elsa said. "He's going to use what he knows one way or another."

"You may be right," Niebohr said. "I'll have to think about it."

"Yes, you do that, Poppa," she said with a sudden smile as she moved back towards the desk. "And now I must go. I've got a date at an interesting little place in fifth-level Denton." She leaned over and kissed him on his forehead.

He took hold of her wrist, sensing the electric warmth of her flesh. "Would I find it interesting?" he asked.

"I wouldn't dream of taking you to such a place," she said grinning. "You might be corrupted."

"Whore!" he said fondly.

She paused once again in the doorway on her way out. "I just remembered, there's a big blonde gets along there who's just your style. I'll ship her over to you gift-wrapped. You look as though you could do with a bit of relaxation."

"There are other kinds, you know," he said.

"Poppa, I do believe you're getting old," Elsa chuckled. "Better take a couple of hormone shots before she arrives, huh?"

Chapter Twenty-one

*When you have eliminated the impossible,
whatever remains, however improbable, must
be the truth.*

CONAN DOYLE

Henry Fong sat in the semi-darkness looking at the
sleek, deadly image of the thing on the screen. He
felt a sudden chill crawl up his spine and blow like
a cold wind from nowhere into his mind, bringing
with it dark, fearful thoughts.

"Have you considered the implications of what you
are saying, Commander Bruce?" he said. "You're quite
sure that there could not be some other explanation
for the presence of this object on Orphelin Three?"

Tom Bruce was standing near the screen, his
strong features partly lit by reflection. "Mr. President,
there is absolutely no doubt at all that what you see
before you is one of the warhead sections of a Mark
IV Dekapod missile."

"*One* of the sections?"

Bruce nodded. "The other nine detonated on impact. Lieutenant Lee, who is a specialist in such matters, believes that the destruction on the northern con-

tinent of Orphelin Three could have been—and most likely was—produced by the patterned delivery of just such a multiple-warhead missile."

Fong found himself still struggling to erect a comforting doubt between himself and the ghastly truth he had already sensed.

"Couldn't the presence of this missile be accounted for in any other way? Some long-forgotten accident, perhaps? I understand that Corps maneuvers were held in that area some ten years ago. Isn't it possible that at that time such an unarmed missile could have gone astray?"

"I'm afraid that has been eliminated quite definitely," Bruce said. "He turned to the young officer who was operating the projector. "Slide fifteen again, please, Lieutenant."

There was a moment's delay, then the general view of the object that had been on the screen was replaced by a closeup. The fluorescent arrow of Bruce's pointer moved over the picture, coming to rest at the beginning of a row of letters and figures stamped into the metal casing.

"These serial numbers give all essential details of the missile concerned," Bruce explained. "It was manufactured some eighteen months ago in the Murmansk munitions plant and allocated to the Corps Central Arsenal in the Urals."

"And after that?" asked Fong.

"According to Central records, the missile is still stockpiled in Bay 16 of the Underground Storage Bunker number 45. However, a physical check was made on my instructions, and it was found that no missile corresponding to these serial numbers was in Bay 16. The officer in charge of the section suggested the possibility of a computer error; he was not, of course, informed of the reason for the inquiry at this time."

"Such an error is possible?"

"Possible—but highly improbable under the circumstances." Bruce's voice was grim.

"And the alternative?"

"Distasteful as it may be, I'm afraid we have to face the fact that the missile was removed from the Central Arsenal by some unauthorized person or persons."

"Stolen, you mean?"

"Either by the use of some forged requisition order, all traces of which were afterwards erased from the records of the section, or with the direct cooperation of the personnel in charge of the Bay at the time."

Fong shifted in his seat. "I find it a very disturbing possibility."

"No less so than I and my colleagues," said Bruce. "Corps Security has begun an exhaustive investigatation of the incident. There have been no concrete results as yet, but such a coup could only have been planned and carried out by someone with a detailed knowledge of Corps procedure. The missile was stolen by someone who knew just what he was doing down to the smallest detail. It seems reasonable to assume that it was stolen for the specific purpose in which it was eventually employed, because there could be no other use for such a weapon."

Fong fought against the sick horror that threatened to paralyze his thought processes. To think of the murder of millions of innocent colonists as being perpetrated by the inhuman aliens known as Kilroys had been terrible enough, but the idea that those people had been deliberately murdered by their own species—this was beyond belief and bearing.

"Thank you, Commander Bruce," he said softly. "You have made your points very clearly."

"Would you like me to run through the slides again?" Bruce asked.

"No. . .no," Fong said. "I've seen quite enough." He turned to the officer by the projector. "Lieutenant—you will please leave us now."

As soon as the young officer had left the room Fong rose to his feet and walked across to the light switches. Commander Bruce was standing quite still next to the dead screen, his strong features grim and his eyes staring unseeing into some other space than that of the luxuriously furnished lounge. Fong had known and respected Bruce for many years, and he understood with some sympathy that recent events had shaken the very foundations of his beliefs, both as a man and a devoted Corps officer.

"Please sit down, Commander," he said. "Can I get you something to drink?"

"No thank you, Mr. President," Bruce said.

The refusal was typical of the man, thought Fong. He would deliberately not dull the edge of the anguish. Fong lowered his spare body into an armchair and gestured to Bruce to do the same.

Bruce obeyed. "I'm sorry, Mr. President, but right now I'm finding it rather difficult to think of anything but one single conclusion. Whichever road I take in my reasoning, I seem to get to the same place, and it's not a place I ever thought I'd be. I trained with Robert Prince for five years, and served with him after that for another three. We were. . . I know it sounds trite—but we were like brothers. I thought I knew him as well as I've ever known any human being."

"A notoriously unreliable breed," said Fong. "It may be a sad judgment, but the older I become, the less I learn to expect from people in matters that truly offer them a free choice. It often seems to me that under such circumstances they are more than fifty percent likely to take the wrong path. But then again, one must bear in mind that even an apparent choice between good and evil is merely a matter of viewpoint in many cases. In a specific instance my good may well be your evil, or vice versa."

Fong watched the expression of alert impatience grow on Bruce's face, and he realized with some satisfaction that his ponderous philosophizing had had the intended effect.

"I'm sorry, Mr. President," Bruce said with a new alertness. "But I can only deal in facts. Abstractions are not my line of country."

"Fine, Commander!" Fong said. "Let's start by my telling you the way the facts look to me. If I get out of line anywhere, I want you to put me right. Understood?"

"Yes, Mr. President."

"Right—we'll start from the beginning. Elkan Niebohr called me to say that there had been a communications break with Orphelin Three for almost two days."

"When such a break should have been reported, under Regulations, within twenty-four hours," Bruce pointed out.

Fong nodded. "But, as I said at the time, Niebohr doesn't lightly call for Corps assistance, not even when his own pet colonial project is involved. Now

. . .some hundred and forty-odd hours later you arrive at Orphelin, to find the entire inhabited northern continent devastated by atomic bombardment, presumably instigated by the aliens we call Kilroys, and you send down a party under the command of Lieutenant Commander Lindstrom to investigate further and to pick up any survivors. While this investigation is going on, *Venturer Twelve* remains in orbit and an apparent UFO is detected approaching the Orphelin system. The alarm proves to be a false one. The UFO is identified as Excelsior Corporation ship *Medusa,* commanded by Robert Prince, who explains that he passed through the Orphelin system only three days previously on his way to Balomain. He says that he has returned upon receiving the alarm call about the breakdown in communications with Orphelin Three, is apparently shocked when you tell him of the destruction of the colony, and offers assistance."

"After suggesting that he should first pick up the team of engineers and geologists he dropped off at Orphelin Four on the way out," interrupted Bruce.

"A suggestion to which you raised no objection?"

"There seemed no reason to do so, particularly as there was a possibility—admittedly remote—that the party on Orphelin Four might be able to give us some information about the presumed Kilroy attack."

"And that was your last contact with *Medusa?*" asked Fong.

"No. Shortly after that I called Prince again to tell him that Lindstrom had at last managed to find a single survivor and that we guessed him to be Mac-Guinness, the biologist whom Prince himself had mentioned."

"An assumption which has since been proved correct, I understand," said Fong. "Although I'm afraid that the reports on the poor fellow's condition are not at all encouraging, even though he is getting the best attention that the staff of the Corps Infirmary can provide. He was still unconscious and completely dependent on artificial life-support systems when I last spoke to Surgeon General Hurwitz."

"George Maseba did his best, but he apparently missed out on some fast-breeding, mutated virus," said Bruce.

"Considering the number of things that were wrong with MacGuinness when we picked him up, that's hardly surprising, but I'm afraid Maseba doesn't see it that way. He's hard on the people who work with him—but he's a great deal tougher on himself."

"Surgeon General Hurwitz has already made it quite clear to me that, with the facilities and the time available to him, Commander Maseba did a first-class job," said Fong. "Without his efforts, MacGuinness would surely have been dead before *Vee Twelve* reached Earth."

"Thank you, Mr. President," Bruce said. "I'll quote you on that, if I may. Although I doubt if it will make George feel any better if the patient doesn't survive."

"And *Medusa* left the Orphelin system how long after that call?" asked Fong.

"Forty minutes—during most of which time she was in the shadow of Orphelin Four, presumably picking up the exploration party," said Bruce. "After that she headed out of the system like a cat with its tail on fire, ignoring all signals from *Vee Twelve*."

"What were your reactions at the time?"

"I was hopping mad, naturally," Bruce said. "Prince knew darned well that in that type of Emergency situation he had no right leaving the system without my permission."

"An uncharacteristic act on the part of Prince, would you say?"

"Completely."

"What happened next?"

"Maybe two minutes later we got this call through from the officer whom Lindstrom had left in charge of the party working on the recovery of the unexploded missile."

"And that call changed your assessment of the entire situation?"

Bruce nodded grimly. "It could hardly do otherwise. I became suddenly aware that what I had automatically assumed to be the work of the Kilroys could be that of some other agency—a human one, in fact."

"And *Medusa*, under the command of Robert Prince, was presumably the last Earth ship to have passed through the area."

Bruce's head bowed, his red hair showing a far greater sprinkling of grey than Fong had ever noticed before. He seemed almost to be talking to himself as he said: "Even when we had the cursed thing on board and battened down in a shielded hold, I kept telling myself that there had to be some other explanation. . ."

"There still could be," Fong said.

"You don't really believe that either, do you?" Bruce said. "When *Medusa* left the Orphelin system I naturally assumed that she was headed back to Earth, to report to Niebohr what had happened on Orphelin Three. Instead she seems to have disappeared from known space. What else can I assume but that

Prince made a bolt for it when he realized that I had stumbled on the truth?"

"Thus making you even more certain of his guilt?" Fong said thoughtfully. "That seems a rather stupid thing to do."

"I agree with you," Bruce said. "I wish to God I could think of some other explanation."

"It does seem that the circumstantial evidence against Prince is very strong. But why would such a man be guilty of this act? The cold-blooded murder of five million people. . ." Fong rose to his feet and walked across to the open window, where he stood looking up into the night sky. It was some time before he spoke again, and when he did so it was in a low voice, almost as though he was vocalizing his thoughts for his own benefit alone.

"I wonder. . .A special kind of man. . .one whose ideals are such that he has always lived in a world that exists mainly in his own imagination—a world where all the people are as good, honest and true as he has always tried to be. And yet, how could such a man exist in our world? If he did, he would surely become disillusioned and embittered, be forced to change his views?"

"Not Bob Prince," Bruce said. "At least during the time I was with him constantly, people seemed to respond to his trust by showing him the better side of their nature. Perhaps it had something to do with his personal charm, but in the main people seemed to live up to his idea of them, and even if they didn't, he would always find some excuse for those who didn't."

The President nodded. "It would be easy to dismiss such a man as some kind of holy fool, except that I know Robert Prince was a great deal more than that. On the other hand, such a personality might well be tipped over the edge of insanity if he was forced to change the views on which his entire life was based. Say, for instance, that he were married to a woman whom he loved completely, uncompromisingly, trusting her without reservation, ignoring any suggestion that she might be something other than the chaste, wonderful creature his romantic idealism leads him to believe? But what if there came a time when the weight of evidence was so overwhelming that even he could not any longer ignore the fact that his ideal woman was a depraved, promiscuous whore who had cuckolded him on numberless occasions? What might such a man do in those circumstances?"

He turned to face Tom Bruce and saw that the Corpsman was staring at him, an expression of acute discomfort on his face.

"I should think he might very well murder her," Bruce said.

"Or destroy something that was associated in his mind with his wife," Fong said. "Some symbolic act that would give him a measure of relief without placing on him the intolerable burden of attacking her personally. Remember, he would still love her, if he was so constant."

"I think perhaps I'll have that drink after all, Mr. President," said Tom Bruce.

Chapter Twenty-two

A man becomes an adult only when he is
able to distinguish his wants from his needs.
JOHN HYNAM—Chief World Congressional
Librarian, Lake Cities.

Elkan Niebohr's office was at the top of the Excelsior Corporation building. An eyrie of stainless steel and glass that looked out over the panorama of Lake Cities, it was served by a private elevator which hummed its way smoothly upwards from the parking lot a hundred and fifty floors below in less than ten seconds. The doors opened with a slight hiss, and Elkan Niebohr stepped out onto the thick purple carpeting of an anteroom guarded over by a tall, grey-haired secretary of forbidding ugliness and complete reliability.

"Good morning, Miss Dalgethy."

"Mr. Niebohr," she acknowledged, looking up from her constantly busy typer. "You have a visitor."

He made a natural assumption. "Elsa here already?"

"No, sir—Doctor Wernher."

Niebohr frowned and hurried through into the

main office. Wernher was standing by the huge computer-controlled wall chart, which provided a constantly changing display of facts and figures about Excelsior holdings. He turned to face his employer, the square features composed.

"Why wasn't I informed that *Medusa* had landed?" demanded Niebohr.

"Because she hasn't," Wernher said evenly. "I came in four hours ago on *Theseus*."

"But Fong told me that *Medusa* had left the Orphelin system."

"She's done that for sure," Wernher said with a quiet arrogance that Niebohr found disconcerting. "What else did Fong tell you?"

"What do you mean?"

"You'd better sit down, Mr. Niebohr," Wernher said. "This may come as something of a shock to you. They found MacGuinness."

Niebohr felt something lurch deep inside his gut. "The biologist—he's alive?"

"Just," said Wernher. "For the time being, at least. He's been unconscious ever since they picked him up, so he hasn't talked yet."

Niebohr lowered himself carefully into a chair. "How could he possibly have survived?"

Wernher shrugged. "I led the mopping-up party myself, and I could have sworn we obliterated that camp of his. But don't worry, I'll get to him before he starts shooting his mouth off. That was one of my reasons for coming back here as soon as possible."

"One of your reasons?"

"There was something else Fong didn't tell you. That smart-assed bastard Bruce knows that Orphelin Three wasn't a Kilroy operation."

"How could he possibly guess that?"

"No guessing—one of the missiles was a dud and his people fished it up. The Corps are hardly likely to miss out on the identification of one of their own weapons."

An explosion of blind, choking rage mushroomed inside Niebohr. "You blundering fool!" He began to raise himself from the chair.

"Steady . . . take it easy," Wernher said soothingly, raising one hand. "The unexploded missile was unfortunate, but it need not be disastrous. The way I've got things figured, you should come up smelling of roses after all—thanks to good old Bob Prince."

This was no bluff, but the cool confidence of a man who had the entire situation under control, he reassured himself. Niebohr's anger subsided slightly.

"Prince—where is Prince?" he asked.

Wernher's solid features broke into a cruel grimace of a smile. "About now I'd say he was due for a spectacular cremation. Last time I saw him he was headed out of the airlock in the direction of a G-type sun, the name of which I couldn't even guess at."

"He's dead?"

"They don't come any deader."

"You killed him?"

"Naturally—to save *your* neck," Wernher said. "Given another few hours, he and his pal Bruce would have blown the whole thing. Now—as far as Bruce is concerned, Prince ran out rather than face the incriminating evidence that was being found on Orphelin Three. I tell you this: Bob Prince is going to be worth a great deal more to you dead than he ever was alive."

"And *Medusa?*"

"I was wondering when you were going to ask that

question," Wernher said. "I'm afraid you're going to lose her too, but the insurance company ought to soften that blow slightly. Right now she's headed out to hell and gone with that lush Coogan in command. I quadrupled his pension, by the way—but don't worry, he won't have time to collect it. Quite soon, *Medusa's* going to have a pretty conclusive accident. My boys will take care of that, then make their way back in their own time aboard the scout ship. Nobody will ever know what happened to *Medusa,* other than the fact that Prince used her to make good his escape."

"You really think Fong and the Corps are going to believe Prince destroyed the Orphelin Three colony?'" said Niebohr.

"What else *can* they believe?"

"But what if they should decide that he did it on my orders?"

"That wouldn't make sense," said Wernher. "Why should you order him to bomb the planet that has been your pride and joy for over twenty years?"

"The only weak link is MacGuinness. If he recovers consciousness and tells what he knows—"

"Relax, Mr. Niebohr. I'll take care of it, just as soon as we've settled one or two points about the future."

Niebohr looked up into the square, arrogant features and realized that he had made certain miscalculations at the outset of this affair. Elsa had been right about Wernher, more right than even she realized. He had allowed himself to be lulled into complacency because of the man's usefulness, but now he saw that Wernher had been playing his own game all along the line. Wernher saw himself as the potential successor to the presidency of Excelsior, but he had known that he could never attain that goal while Prince was still around. Strange that neither he nor Prince appeared to realize that the true, natural successor was Elsa.

A pity about Prince. . .Elsa wouldn't like it at all. If she found out the truth, he had no doubt that she would tear Wernher apart with her own delicate claws, tough as he was. But there was no point in Elsa being involved in Wernher's disposal—as she herself had said, there were other hatchet men. Better for the time being that Robert Prince should remain in her mind as the missing hero.

"We'll talk about the future *after* you've finished off the job you started," he said firmly. "Just so long as MacGuinness stays alive there may be no future."

"For you, maybe—but nobody even knows I was on board *Medusa*," Wernher said.

Niebohr sighed inwardly. Impatience and greed. . . Such lack of subtlety. . . "Kurt, you have my word, you'll get everything you deserve. But first clean up this MacGuinness business. You may be in the clear personally, but he could ruin the entire Corporation —and that would hardly be in your interest, would it?"

"All right," Wernher said. "Although I think you're panicking unnecessarily. Even when MacGuinness does regain consciousness, there's no reason why he should immediately start chirping about this mutation thing. There are going to be other things on his mind besides that."

"You may be right—but I want it settled right now."

"It shall be done!" Wernher clicked his heels with a hint of arrogant mockery and left the room.

Niebohr waited for a few moments until he heard

the muted hiss of the closing doors of the elevator, then he switched on his intercom.

"Miss Dalgethy—get me Chandos right away, will you?"

Admiral Karl Hurwitz was a big man with the round, ruddy-cheeked face of a prosperous butcher. Wernher looked at the great sausage-like fingers and thought contemptuously that only an organization like the Corps could ever have promoted such an oaf to the high position of Surgeon General.

"No. . .Doctor Wernher, I have given due consideration to your request, and I'm afraid that under the circumstances it is out of the question," Hurwitz said. "Professor MacGuinness's condition is extremely serious, and he is receiving the best treatment we can provide—"

"Precisely my point," cut in Wernher, deliberately smiling at a point beyond the Surgeon General's left shoulder. Through the window behind the desk he could see out over the sunlit roofs of the massive Corps Infirmary to the blue of the Pacific Ocean beyond. "Mr. Niebohr feels a special responsibility towards Professor MacGuinness, who is a valued employee, and he is determined to carry out his obligations to the full. He believes that the Professor's interests would best be served by transferring him to a private nursing home where he would receive personal attention."

"Even if I could accept the suggestion that this nursing home of yours was capable of providing for the special needs of the patient, I would still not consider sanctioning his transfer," said Hurwitz firmly. "Such a move would surely kill him."

"My dear Admiral, how can you possibly expect

me to believe that?" said Wernher with deliberate insolence. "MacGuinness survived the transfer from *Venturer Twelve* to this infirmary—and he has been experiencing the benefits of what you yourself described as 'the best treatment' since then. Surely it is reasonable to assume that he should be this time be considerably stronger?"

"You should know, *Doctor* Wernher, that medicine is not always quite so predictable," said Hurwitz. "Professor MacGuinness was suffering from a bewildering variety of symptoms, some of which were masking others and making the task of diagnosis almost impossible."

"I see," Wernher said. "And can we take it that now the patient is receiving the treatment he really needs?"

"You will have to accept my word that that is the case," Hurwitz said.

"And the prognosis?"

"There seems to me no reason to suppose that he will not eventually recover completely—but it will be a long process."

"And his condition at this moment?" pursued Wernher.

"He is as well as can be expected."

"Oh now, come on Admiral," Wernher said derisively. "You're not talking to some dumb relative. I've heard all the platitudes before—used them myself."

"The patient is unconscious and he is being fed intravenously," Hurwitz said stiffly. "At the moment a heart/lung life-support system is backing up his natural resources, and he is also undergoing dialysis every eight hours to rid his system of the waste products produced by our measures against his multiple infections."

"In other words, he's in pretty bad shape—despite your so-called 'best treatment,'" Wernher said. He rose to his feet, his grey eyes flat and threatening as he stared at Hurwitz. "And I want to tell you this, Admiral. Mr. Niebohr isn't going to be at all happy if anything goes wrong. Should MacGuinness die, he will most surely take out an action for negligence against yourself and the Corps Infirmary."

The color of Karl Hurwitz's pink cheeks deepened. "You can tell your Mr. Niebohr that in the event of any such thing happening he can take his action against me personally. I shall take the greatest pleasure in defending myself against any accusations you may care to make. In the meantime, do me the favor of getting the hell out of my office and my hospital!"

"Am I to take it that you are denying me, as Mr. Niebohr's personal medical representative, the opportunity of making an independent examination of the patient?" Wernher said. "I would remind you that I have a legal right to do so—which can be enforced if necessary by an injunction."

"Very well, Doctor Wernher," said Hurwitz. "I will give instructions to the physician in charge that you are to be allowed to examine Professor MacGuinness. But I warn you that if any attempt is made to remove him from my care at this time you will find yourself facing charges of unprofessional conduct."

"Thank you, Admiral," Wernher said, inclining his head in deliberate mockery. "I shall make it my business to inform Mr. Niebohr of your courteous cooperation. And now, if you will call someone to conduct me to the patient?"

Chapter Twenty-three

The Statesman lives with his failures—
the Doctor buries his.

The Wit and Wisdom
of Henry Fong (p. 235)

"I know you think I'm obsessional about this kind of thing, but I like to follow a case through," said George Maseba as Tom Bruce brought the flycar in for a landing on the parking lot of the Corps Infirmary. "In any case, I feel kind of guilty that I didn't sort out that virus infection of MacGuinness's while we were on the way back to Earth."

"You did the best you could under the circumstances," said Bruce. "Hurwitz himself said you did a good job."

Maseba's dark face was solemn. "There's only one good job in medicine—and that's the one that gives the patient a one hundred percent cure."

"You sure don't let up on yourself, do you?" Tom Bruce said as he flipped open the canopy of the flycar and the two of them stepped out onto the concrete. "We just lost five million people out there and you're worrying about one man."

"That's what matters in medicine," Maseba said as they walked toward the reception entrance. "The really important factor is the personal relationship between physician and patient."

Under any other circumstances Bruce might have made some remark about Maseba's semi-mystical approach to his vocation having archetypal roots in his ancestral African past, but he sensed that any of the tired old cracks about witch doctors that he and Lindstrom occasionally made when kidding Maseba would be in the very worst possible taste at this time.

"You may be right," he said mildly, "but I think you can take it that Hurwitz and his staff will be doing the very best they can. It often seems to me that—" He stopped talking as he realized that Maseba was no longer walking at his side.

The medic was standing about three meters back, watching a stockily built man in dark-grey civilian clothes who was walking in the direction of a bright yellow flycar parked near to the one they had just left.

"Hey, George!" Bruce shouted. "Are you with me?"

The car lifted into the air and headed off, gathering speed, in an easterly direction. Maseba turned, his expression troubled.

"Sorry. . . But there was something so familiar about that guy. I'm sure I should know him from somewhere."

Bruce shook his head, grinning. "What I prescribe for you, Doctor, is a few weeks' quiet leave."

"I might just take you up on that," Maseba said,

falling into step beside him as they walked into Reception. "But not until the MacGuinness case is cleared up."

They stepped into a waiting elevator and traveled fifteen floors down in silence.

"I'm pleased you know your way around this labyrinth," said Bruce. "I'm lost already." They left the elevator and walked through pastel-shaded corridors paved with resilient, sound-absorbing plastic.

"I should—I spent five years here," Maseba said. "That was before Hurwitz took over, of course." They rounded a corner and found themselves facing a pair of doors marked: INTENSIVE CARE SECTION— NO ADMITTANCE.

"Ah, here we are," Maseba said, thrusting his Medical Officer's key-card into the scanner.

Two white-uniformed orderlies were standing in the corridor beyond, talking beside a stretcher trolley. They stiffened to attention as the two officers approached.

Bruce followed Maseba as he walked straight on past the orderlies and pushed open the door of a ward.

"I thought I told—?" the voice of a harassed-looking young Medic Lieutenant died away as he recognized the intruder. "Oh, it's you, Commander."

"What's happening here?" demanded Maseba.

As far as Bruce was concerned the room appeared to be in a state of chaos. Three doctors were bending over the figure on the bed, while several orderlies hovered in the background, either watching or making adjustments to the batteries of electronic gadgetry that cluttered the floor and walls of the room.

"We're trying a revivification, sir, but I'm afraid the outlook isn't good—brain damage must be pretty far advanced," said the lieutenant.

"But that's impossible!" Maseba said. "The life-support system should be capable of keeping him going indefinitely. You would have had ample warning—"

"I know, sir," said the lieutenant unhappily. "But an unfortunate combination of circumstances. . . The heart-lung machine must have malfunctioned—we suspect a cerebral embolism—but matters were made worse by the fact that the monitoring system didn't give the alarm as it should have done. . ."

Maseba thrust past the lieutenant and joined the group around the pallid, bearded figure on the bed. Bruce, afflicted by the usual layman's feelings of helplessness under such circumstances, stood by watching as instruments and orders were passed back and forth.

Several minutes later, George Maseba, his face gleaming like wet ebony, threw a used hypodermic from him in a gesture of disgust. "There's nothing more we can do for him," he said, turning away from the bed. "Better report to the Surgeon General, Lieutenant."

"Yes, sir," said the young lieutenant unhappily. "I just can't understand it, sir. He was doing fine when Doctor Wernher was here—the whole system working perfectly. I thought at the—"

"Doctor. . .*What was that name?*" demanded Maseba sharply.

"Wernher, sir," said the lieutenant. "The aide who brought him down from the Admiral's office said he was the personal representative of Mr. Niebohr, president of the Excelsior Colonization Corporation. The

Surgeon General gave him clearance to examine the patient."

"I see. And who was present while he made that examination—you?"

"Why yes, sir. . ."

"The whole time?"

"Well, sir, there was a call for me on Ward F. . ."

"All right, Lieutenant, carry on," Maseba said. He turned to Bruce. "Come on, Tom, there's nothing more we can do here."

Maseba maintained a stony silence as they walked back along the corridor toward the elevator. Bruce made no attempt to question him—he knew the signs of one of Maseba's constructive rages from way back. Sometimes he would go into one of these waking trances for maybe ten, fifteen minutes, not speaking until he had synthesized the whole problem in his mind.

"Back to base?" he said as they stepped out of the elevator on the Reception floor.

Maseba nodded.

They had been in the air some ten minutes when he spoke at last.

"Kurt Wernher," he said, his voice grating on the name. "I knew I'd seen him somewhere before. It must be all of fifteen years, but I couldn't miss that arrogant swagger and those eyes—like grey stones."

"Wernher?" Bruce glanced at his companion.

"The guy who boarded that yellow flycar just as we were walking into Reception," Maseba said.

"Then you did know him?"

"We were in pre-med together up in Montreal," Maseba said. "I often wondered what happened to him."

"Personal representative of Niebohr—he must have done well for himself," Bruce said.

"That figures. He would be where the loot was. Even as a kid he was always hustling. There was some trouble with the Dope Squad, I remember, but nothing was ever pinned on him."

Bruce eyed the seething, obvious rage on the face of his companion. "George—what really happened to MacGuinness?"

"He must have been in the way, poor bastard," Maseba said bitterly.

"In the way—of what?"

"I can't even begin to guess."

"Are you suggesting that Wernher murdered him?"

"You'd never prove it in court in a million years," Maseba said. "On the face of it MacGuinness was the victim of an unusual, but quite explicable, set of circumstances—a malfunction of the life-support system which would have been corrected if the monitor alarm hadn't failed at the same time. A million to one shot. . ."

"But you don't believe it was that way?"

"If Wernher was alone in that ward with MacGuinness for several minutes, he would have had time to fix a dozen such accidents," Maseba said. "A patient dependent on such a life-support system is completely vulnerable. The turn of a dial, a slight mechanical adjustment, an imbalance of pressure—any one of a thousand small things can kill him. Make no mistake about it, Wernher would know that."

Bruce found the whole concept deeply shocking. "But he's a doctor, George!"

"Now who's being mystical?" Maseba said. "What makes you think that doctors are any different from other human beings? I suppose you think that we're all bloody Florence Nightingales—devoted to relieving the ills of suffering humanity, and all that floop? I tell you something, friend: Doctors come in all shapes, sizes and colors—and with all kinds of motivations. Money, power, sex, vanity—you name it and there's some medic somewhere using that kind of fuel."

"And Wernher?"

"The first four would fit like a glove, from what I recall of him."

"And you intend to let him get away with this?"

"Tom, don't be naïve. There just isn't a darned thing I can do about it. I already explained that," said Maseba patiently. "In my profession, a good way to drive yourself out of your skull is to start worrying over the kinds of things you can't do anything about."

"That's one way of looking at it," Tom Bruce said. "But I was trained in the Junius Carter school of tactics. We don't give up so easily."

"Using your head as a battering ram can be a mite painful at times," said Maseba, with the suggestion of a grin.

"That depends on the thickness of the head and the nature of the problem," Bruce said. "Let me put it to you this way—although there's apparently no way of proving it, we're pretty certain that Wernher deliberately killed MacGuinness, right?"

"I'd say so. But where does that get you?"

"It gets me hopping mad, and darned curious," Bruce said. "Both MacGuinness and Wernher are employees of Niebohr. MacGuinness was doing some kind of research on Orphelin Three, wasn't he?"

"Connected with fish, I believe."

"Uh-huh. . . And as chance would have it, he was the only survivor when the planet was blasted. Now why would Niebohr want him dead too?"

"Now just a minute—where do you get that *too?*" said Maseba. "You're implying that Bob Prince destroyed the Orphelin colony on orders from Niebohr?"

Bruce frowned. "No. . .that doesn't make any more sense than Henry Fong's idea that he bombed the planet because he had gone insane. I don't think Bob Prince was capable of committing such an act under any circumstances."

"Then what really happened?"

"I don't know. . .yet," Bruce said. "But I'm sure as hell going to find out."

Chapter Twenty-four

It is no more reasonable to assume that all the processes involved in government should be exposed to the common gaze than to suppose it desirable that the human body should remain nude in all social situations. While it might prove interesting, even titillating in some cases, I can think of many instances when even the least prudish person might well be offended by such indiscriminate exposure.

*The Wit and Wisdom
of Henry Fong (p. 879)*

Helen Lindstrom shook her head. "I think you're letting this thing get out of proportion, Tom," she said. "Why not accept the evidence as it stands and admit that Bob Prince must have been responsible for the destruction of Orphelin Three?"

"Because it just doesn't fit in with the character of Prince as I know him," Bruce said vehemently. The two of them were sitting in the small lounge of his quarters at Melpond Base. Lindstrom had arrived some ten minutes earlier to collect her orders for the administration of the still-grounded *Venturer Twelve*.

"That may be where you're making your mistake,"

Helen said, turning the moisture-beaded glass of Campari and soda carefully between her long pale fingers. "It seems to me that the Robert Prince you once knew may no longer exist. Life and circumstances change people. How can you honestly go on trying to kid yourself that working for Elkan Niebohr and married to that bitch Elsa would have no effect whatever on a man?"

"You'll be telling me next that you believe Fong's theory."

"No, not really—and I don't think he does either," Helen said.

"Now what is that supposed to mean?" he said sharply.

She looked at him, a fond tolerance in her eyes. "You know, Tom—guys like you and Bob Prince—sometimes I wonder if you ever live in the world as it really is."

Bruce bit back an angry reply as the vidphone chimed. Walking across to the instrument, he pressed the connecting button. The moustached face of Delgado appeared. He was a senior operative of SCRUTATOR, a private intelligence agency of high reputation.

"Commander Bruce—can we talk?"

"Sure—go ahead."

"We've been checking on your boy Wernher," Delgado said. "Seems that before his landing from *Theseus* he was off Earth for approximately eight days, but so far nobody seems to know where. One thing for sure, he wasn't on Maxwell Two, where *Theseus* came from. *Theseus* is the only ship to have hit there in over three months."

"In that case he must have boarded her in transit to Earth."

Delgado nodded. "That's the way we figured it. We followed up—discreetly of course—and found that when *Theseus* landed she was carrying more than her normal complement of lifeboats. A check showed that one of these had been used recently, and further examination made it obvious that the original ship's name had been removed and replaced by that of *Theseus*."

Bruce felt a growing excitement. At last he was getting somewhere. "Can you find out what that old name was?"

"We already have," Delgado said. "Does the name *Medusa* ring any bells with you?"

"By God it does!" exclaimed Bruce. "Have you located Wernher yet?"

Delgado frowned. "No—he seems to be lying pretty low. Nobody's seen him around for over twenty-four hours now. In fact, our last positive sighting seems to be when you and Maseba saw him leaving the Corps Infirmary."

"When you do find him, bring him in right away," Bruce said.

"On what charges?"

"Just bring him in—we'll figure the rest later," Bruce said.

"A cookie like this Wernher isn't going to crumble the minute you speak harshly to him. Maybe it would be better to hold off for a while and keep him under close surveillance."

"Bring him in!"

Delgado shrugged. "All right, Commander, you're the boss. I'll call you the moment we've got him."

"Do that." Bruce broke the connection and turned to Helen, a flush of triumph on his face. "We're really beginning to get somewhere at last."

"You think that Wernher was aboard *Medusa* when she left on that last trip?" Helen asked.

"He must have been."

"And now he's back on Earth—but Prince and *Medusa* are where?"

"Wernher knows—he just *has* to."

"You're only guessing."

"Maybe so—but it makes a hell of a lot more sense to suppose that Wernher was the brains behind the Orphelin Three massacre than it does to pin the blame on Bob Prince."

"But Prince was still in command of *Medusa*," Helen pointed out. "You can't ignore that fact. If the attack was launched from *Medusa* he must have known about it."

Bruce turned in the act of pouring himself another scotch on the rocks. "Sure, provided the missile *was* launched from *Medusa*."

Helen frowned. "How's that? You just lost me."

"You remember that team of geologists and engineers Prince said he dropped off on Orphelin Four?"

"Yes. Prince went to pick them up just before he headed *Medusa* out of the Orphelin system."

"I expect that, like me, you assumed that he had landed them directly onto the planetary surface?"

"Naturally. . ."

"Not really, when you come to consider it," Bruce said. "In fact, it would be a costly exercise in time, fuel, and effort for a ship like *Medusa*. Those geologists—if that's what they really were—could have gone in under their own power, using some small craft that had been transported to the Orphelin system aboard *Medusa*."

"A scout ship, for instance?" Helen said.

"Sure, why not? *Medusa's* hold could take six at least."

"Supposing you're right—what then?"

"Surely it's obvious," Bruce said. "A scout ship would be quite capable of carrying a Dekapod missile, and there would be no way that Prince could know of its existence unless he actually went aboard looking for it. He would just drop the scout off— Wernher would be in charge of it, of course—and head on towards Balomain, completely unaware of what was going to happen."

"You really are determined that Bob Prince should come out of this thing white as snow, aren't you?" Helen said. "But even if we agree on your assumption that Wernher was the one who actually delivered the missile, there are still a lot of things that need explaining. For a starter—why was the Orphelin Three colony destroyed, and on whose orders?"

"The answer to that just has to be Elkan Niebohr," Bruce said unhappily. "But at the moment I must confess I just can't begin to imagine why. Orphelin Three was Niebohr's baby, his pride and joy— the finest single property on the books of Excelsior. It just doesn't make sense."

"Neither does the disappearance of Prince and *Medusa*," Helen said. "If he's as completely innocent as you maintain he is, why would he run away?"

Bruce shook his head. "I don't think we're going to know any of those answers until we find Wernher."

"And maybe not even then, if he's as tough a proposition as your friend Delgado appears to believe," Helen said.

He was working over the draft of his script when Miss Dalgethy called to say that Elsa was in the outer office. "All right—send her in," he said, thrusting the loose sheets into a drawer of his desk.

He looked up with pleasure as she walked towards him across the thick purple lawn of the carpet. She was wearing a deep emerald town suit of some metallic, glittering material, with matching shoes and shoulder bag.

"Hallo, baby," he said, smiling indulgently. "You look like something right off the front page of *Fashion Flair*."

"You say the nicest things," she said, placing a wet kiss on the top of his bald head before perching on the edge of the desk like a bright, beautiful bird. "Poppa. . ."

Her use of the "little girl" tone that she customarily employed to make some outrageous request alerted him.

"I'm lonesome, Poppa," she said. "When will Bob be coming back?"

So that was it. . . He sighed inwardly, thinking that he would never really understand the female mind.

"Baby, I explained to you already," he said patiently. "It's best for the time being, at least, that he should keep out of the way."

"But why?"

"Now Elsa, you're not that dumb," he said. "If he were to come back now he would have to answer Bruce's charges that he disobeyed orders in an emergency situation."

"I don't see how that can be. The President hasn't even announced the existence of such a situation."

"Not yet—but he won't be able to hold off much longer."

"I can't figure it," Elsa said. "Bob must have known what he was risking when he ran out on Bruce. Why didn't he just sit there and play it cool?"

"Maybe he thought that Bruce's investigations were getting a bit too near the truth."

She frowned. "Now just a minute, Poppa. Are you suggesting that Bob knew the truth himself?"

He shook his head, smiling. "You know, baby— sometimes I think you take this belief in Robert Prince's pristine innocence a bit far. He isn't really that naïve. I'll admit he didn't like the idea at first, but in the long run he saw that it was a matter of survival for all of us."

"You mean he agreed to the destruction of the colony?"

"Didn't *you?*"

"That's different—I'm your daughter."

"Then you should be smart enough to know that conscience takes a back seat when those kinds of stakes are involved."

"He couldn't have kept it from me," she said.

"Do you really think your knight in shining armor would dream of telling such dreadful truths to his beloved and innocent little wife?" Niebohr said. "Especially after I'd sworn him to secrecy?"

"I don't like the idea of his deceiving me, even if he was trying to spare my feelings," she said sulkily.

Niebohr chuckled. "You've kept one or two things from him fairly successfully in your time."

"Pig!" she said, sliding off the edge of the desk and alighting on the floor. "That's a different thing altogether. A girl's got to have some hobbies."

He grinned. "You mean you've found *another?*"

"Oh, there's no bloody sense in you this morning," she snapped. "What the hell are you so self-satisfied about?"

"All in good time, baby—all in good time."

"That does it!" she said, turning and walking quickly towards the door of the room.

"Baby!" he called.

She turned her head sharply, looking at him over her shoulder. "Yes?"

"Just trust Poppa—and if you're not too busy try to catch tonight's *Voice of the Planets* program."

"That public relations crap?" she said disgustedly.

"Steel yourself just this once," he said. "I think you'll find it worthwhile."

Tom Bruce threw the report onto Helen Lindstrom's desk with a gesture of disgust. "What the hell's happening here?" he demanded angrily. "Fifteen crewmen on sick report and four on charges ranging from drunkenness to insubordination."

Helen Lindstrom sighed. "Quite frankly, Tom, the sooner we get *Vee Twelve* out into space again the happier I'll be. We've been grounded here over a week, and I can only keep the crew occupied by inventing maintenance jobs that they've done a dozen times already. You know very well what that kind of meaningless activity can do to morale. We're on Earth, but not on leave. That's the trouble."

"We're running a Corps ship here, not an entertainment center," Bruce said.

"You mean *I'm* running a ship, don't you?" Helen said. "You're too busy playing detective over this Orphelin Three business and Prince to take any real notice of what's happening aboard *Vee Twelve.*"

He ceased his angry pacing and looked down at her, realizing that there was some justification in her reproach. "All right—what do you suggest?"

"Well, at least let me prepare some kind of leave roster. That will give them something to look forward to."

"No—that's impossible. Nobody is to leave base until the President has made his statement about Orphelin Three. We can't run the risk of there being a premature leak."

"I can understand that," Helen said. "But how much longer can he possibly sit on the thing? Surely the media will soon start to get curious?"

"He'll keep them quiet," Bruce said. "In the meantime—" He broke off as the vid on Helen's desk beeped.

"Lieutenant Commander Lindstrom here," she said, flicking the switch. "Yes, he's right here. Hold on." She looked up at Bruce. "It's for you." She vacated the chair as Bruce moved hurriedly around to the other side of the desk and recognized the face of Delgado in the screen.

"Yes?" he said eagerly.

"We found Wernher," said the security man.

"You did? That's fine!" Bruce's spirits lifted. "Have you got him there? When can I talk to him?"

"We don't have him," Delgado said. "And I'm afraid you won't get to talk to him."

"What do you mean?"

"He's in the Second-Level Morgue out at Malton," explained Delgado. "The police found him floating in an ornamental lake early this morning with the back of his head smashed in. They diagnosed a mugging. I haven't disillusioned them."

"Niebohr?" Bruce said.

Delgado shrugged. "Who else? Poppa doesn't believe in nursing liabilities. Wernher had done all that was required of him, and he knew too much."

"Do you think there's any chance of proving a connection?"

"With Poppa Niebohr? Commander, you've just got to be joking. Any other leads you want us to follow up?"

Bruce shook his head. "Not at the moment. I'll be in touch if anything comes up."

"You do that, Commander," Delgado said. "Sorry we couldn't be more help."

Bruce switched off and looked up at Helen, who was standing watching him. "You heard?"

"No more than I expected," she said. "Look, Tom, why don't you just give up? MacGuinness dead, Wernher dead—I'd say it was ninety-five percent certain that Bob Prince must have gone the same way, most probably at the hands of Wernher. And whatever you do isn't going to change that."

"Maybe not, but at least I might be able to make sure that his reputation comes out of this thing in one piece."

"That will be a big consolation to him—and his dear widow."

"Elsa. . .that bitch!" growled Bruce. "How could she let Niebohr do that to her own husband?"

"How do you know she did?" Helen asked.

He looked at her, frowning. "What do you mean?"

"Just that the impression I got back at the Presidential reception was that she was pretty fond of the guy."

"Aw now come on, Helen," he said incredulously. "That same night she was busy promoting her hot little arse into bed with me."

"So?"

"Well, a woman doesn't do that kind of thing if she's in love with her husband."

"She doesn't? Look Tom—you're a fine Corps Commander, but what you know about women isn't worth a damn—especially women like Elsa Niebohr. You were just another stud for her collection—Bob Prince was her husband."

"But she was cheating on him—not just with me."

"Sure she was, but I'm trying to tell you—that wouldn't make any difference as far as she was concerned."

"You mean she could love him and at the same time be making a fool of him? But what if he found out?"

"That's the sauce that adds flavor to the dish," Helen said. "Although I don't think the risk was ever too great. A woman like Elsa would be far too clever to ever let him find her out—and if he suspected her, well, that might be just another way of keeping a tighter hold on him."

"God! You make it sound like some kind of perverted game."

"Poor Tom," she said, smiling at him. "You had a lucky escape, didn't you? If that emergency call hadn't come through, our little Elsa would have eaten you alive, make no mistake about that."

"Rubbish!" he said uncomfortably. "But you've given me an idea."

"Like what?"

"Well, if my suspicions are correct, and Wernher did kill Prince, Elsa's not going to be happy about it, is she?"

"I'd say she'd be hopping mad."

He nodded. "That's the way I figure it." He reached out towards the vid switch. "You'd better keep out of sight of the scanner while I make this call," he said.

Chapter Twenty-five

*To congratulate a man of probity upon his
probity is to offer him a deadly insult.*

*The Wit and Wisdom
of Henry Fong (p. 173)*

She was in the water when he arrived, her lithe
brown body outlined against the pale blue of the
pool bottom as she swam gracefully towards him
beneath the surface. Bursting upwards in a flurry of
bubbles, she extended one arm.

"Nice to see you again, Commander. Haul me, will
you?"

He grasped her wrist and pulled her up onto the
side. She stood grinning at him as she squeezed the
water from her jet black hair with both hands, the
drops glistening on her dark, oiled body like dia-
monds.

"You're going to be kind of hot in that uniform,"
she said. "Why don't you peel?"

"I'm fine as I am, thanks." Bruce was uncomfortably
aware of the echoes of passion that were reawaken-
ing in him at the sight of her nakedness.

199

"You really do want to *talk?*" Her dark eyes regarded him mockingly. "Now that seems an awful waste of a beautiful afternoon."

He stared at her, conscious of his awkwardness and wondering if he had made a mistake in coming here. Back on *Vee Twelve,* what Helen had said seemed to make sense—but here, in Elsa Prince's presence, he had the feeling that even another woman as intelligent as Helen could hardly be expected to predict the reactions of this elemental creature.

"Look, if you're bashful, I'm sure there must be an odd pair of Bob's trunks kicking around in that dressing room," she said. "Why don't you take a look?"

"I don't intend to borrow anything belonging to Bob this trip," he said stiffly.

"My!" she exclaimed with a chuckle. "What happened to my hard-riding Commander? They been feeding you—what do they call them in the good old Corps—Anti Pills?"

"For God's sake, Elsa! I came here for a serious discussion. Can't you stop joking around for just ten minutes?"

She looked up at him as she smoothed the palms of both her hands gently down over her breasts, following the smooth tautness of her flat stomach until they came to rest side by side over the dark vee of her mons pubis.

"This is no joke, Commander. You should know that. Or did they clean out your memory too?"

"Elsa, what I have to talk about is important to both of us, but if you're not going to be sensible I shall just leave."

Her mocking expression hardened, and it seemed to him for a moment as though Elkan Niebohr was staring at him out of those dark eyes. He found himself wondering what she would look like when she was old. He had a sudden vision of a wizened, monkey-like creature of incredible ugliness—as if the corruption that was inside her had gradually externalized itself, imprisoning her in a husk of evil. What if the sensual demands of her body outlived her present beauty? Perhaps she herself saw the same vision, and her present insatiability was in fact a pathetic attempt to store up sexual pleasure against that long winter of neglect.

"All right, Bruce—I don't beg," she said harshly. She picked up a light toweling robe from the lounging bed and slipped it on. "Now, what do you want to talk about?" She sat down on one of the chairs around the umbrella-shaded table.

"Not what—*whom*," he said, lowering himself into the seat opposite her. "Your husband—Bob Prince."

"Your old buddy—the one you're aiming to have grounded."

"Poppa told you about that, did he?"

"Naturally."

"I wonder what else he told you," Bruce said carefully. "I think maybe there were one or two things he left out."

"For instance?" Her dark eyes watched him alertly.

"Like the fact that we're now a hundred percent certain that the destruction of the Orphelin Three colony was not the work of the Kilroys."

"What has that got to do with Bob?" she asked.

"Well, for a starter, all the evidence points to the fact that *Medusa*, under Bob's command, was the last ship known to be in the Orphelin system before the attack. And added to that, his complete familiarity with the type of weapon used."

She shook her head gently. "He just isn't capable of

doing a thing like that. Five million people blotted out."

"I'm talking about the evidence," Bruce said carefully. "Right now, the way Henry Fong has it figured, Bob Prince is the prime candidate. The guilt has to be laid somewhere—and Bob isn't here to defend himself."

"You don't believe Bob killed that planet any more than I do," she said.

"What I believe has nothing to do with it," Bruce said. "Do you know where Bob is now?"

"I haven't the slightest idea," she said. "And if I had I sure wouldn't tell you."

"But you want him back?"

"He's my husband."

"That doesn't answer my question."

"It does as far as I'm concerned," she said, smoothing the robe over her thighs.

"Hasn't it occurred to you that he may have gone the same way as Wernher and MacGuinness?"

She looked up sharply. "Wernher?"

"Didn't Poppa tell you he was back?"

She made a quick recovery. "Maybe. . .I don't remember."

"He went out with *Medusa* on that last trip, didn't he?"

"If you know so much, why do you need any answers from me?" Elsa said.

"If you didn't know he was back on Earth, I don't suppose you knew that he was dead either—on your father's orders after he had disposed of MacGuinness, who was the last remaining link with the Orphelin Three operation?"

"You'd have a hard time proving any of that. In any case, I don't see—"

"Shall I tell you what I think happened?"

"If it amuses you," she said. Her eyes were wary, showing both doubt and deep concern.

"I think that the destruction of Orphelin Three was deliberately planned by your father and Wernher, *without* the knowledge of Bob Prince. I don't think he had the slightest idea what was going on. He believed your father's cover story that he was to transport a group of geologists and engineers for a survey of Orphelin Four, then carry on to Balomain. What neither your father nor Wernher had counted on was the fact that Bob was constantly monitoring Corps frequencies, and that he would turn back to the Orphelin system as soon as he picked up the Emergency call. He would never even have known about the group on Four, if he hadn't. . .and he would probably have been alive today—on Balomain."

"Alive?" she looked up at him, startled.

"Ask yourself this question," Bruce pursued. "What would be Bob Prince's reaction when he found out that he had been used in such a plot? Wernher would *have* to kill him, just as he came back to Earth to kill MacGuinness—and just as your father had Wernher himself killed in his turn."

"You don't know any of this is true—you're just guessing," she said.

"I wouldn't be if you told me why Poppa wanted his pride and joy, Orphelin Three, destroyed," Bruce said.

She regarded him, her head tilted slightly to one side. "Nice try, Commander. In a kind of a way I believe you really do care about Bob and what may have happened to him." She rose to her feet. "You're right, too—I could give you Poppa's head on a plate if

I wanted. But I'm not going to—because Poppa and me—we're family. Now get out!" She turned abruptly and walked swiftly back towards the house. And to Bruce her walk was as confident as ever.

Chapter Twenty-six

On the subject of History again—it may be a comforting thought to remember that evil actions have sometimes produced great good in the long run.

The Wit and Wisdom of Henry Fong (p. 457)

"I really don't think you should blame yourself too much, Commander Bruce," said President Fong.

Tom Bruce shook his head. "I should have known better than to attempt it, but with Wernher dead, tackling Elsa seemed to be the only way."

"You must be right about Prince, of course," Fong said, clinking the ice in his glass of lemon soda. "If he were alive, he would have been back on Earth by now."

"I've been wondering if Elsa knew all along that he might be killed," Bruce said.

Fong shrugged. "She may well have decided he was expendable."

"What kind of woman could think that way about her own husband?"

"We're talking about a female version of Elkan Nie-bohr, and you ask that question?" Fong glanced at his wristwatch. "Excuse me just a moment." He walked over to the big wall-screen vid and switched it on.

A surge of martial music with resounding brass filled the large lounge, then faded slightly as the program title was repeated by the voice of an off-screen announcer.

"Once again *The Voice of the Planets* speaks to the peoples of United Earth. Tonight we begin with an important statement by the President of the Excelsior Colonization Corporation, Mr. Elkan Niebohr."

As the titles faded and dissolved into the scene of an oak-paneled study, the camera zoomed in slowly on the massive figure seated behind the desk. Niebohr's beaked face was solemn.

"Good evening, my friends. I speak to you on this occasion with a mixture of sadness and pride, which I am sure you will all understand when you hear what I have to say. I want to tell you about a planet—a near-paradise where happy colonists have lived and worked under the benevolent guiding hand of the Excelsior Corporation for over twenty years. I speak, of course, of Orphelin Three, whose development I can in all modesty say has been in large measure due to my own personal interest. Any father must have favorites among his children, and I am not ashamed to say that Orphelin Three and its five million inhabitants has always been near to my heart.

"Under these circumstances you will be able to imagine the pain and distress with which I have to tell you that the colony on Orphelin Three no longer exists—that it has been wantonly and wickedly destroyed by the action of those inhuman creatures we have come to call Kilroys. Some ten days ago there was a sudden break in communications. . ."

"For God's sake, Mr. President!" exclaimed Bruce. "Did you know about this?"

"Later, Commander, later," said Fong, waving one hand in a gesture that demanded silence.

". . .First on the scene was the Corps ship *Venturer Twelve,* under the command of Commander Thomas Winford Bruce, who immediately initiated a full-scale rescue operation in the hope of saving any survivors of the holocaust. Shortly after that, the Excelsior Corporation freighter *Medusa,* under the command of our fleet director—my own son-in-law, Commander Robert Prince—arrived and offered assistance to Commander Bruce, comrade of the days when he too was a member of the Corps. However, while discussions of the form this assistance might best take were still going on, the radar operator of *Medusa* reported the appearance of a UFO in the area of the outer planets of the Orphelin system. Realizing that *Venturer Twelve* was fully occupied with the rescue operation, Commander Prince paused only long enough to send a brief message to his Corps colleague before heading off at full acceleration to investigate the UFO."

Niebohr paused for a long moment before continuing, his deep-set eyes staring into the camera. "Some of you may not understand the kind of courage implied by an act of that nature—the sheer selfless determination to serve and to avenge in some measure the sufferings of his fellow human beings that led Bob Prince, commanding an unarmed merchant ship, to take off in pursuit of a deadly enemy. Such men are not of common clay—they are a special breed. In the event, we can only guess at the outcome, because both *Medusa* and the UFO she was pursuing soon disappeared beyond range of *Venturer Twelve's* detection equipment, and neither has been sighted since. It may be that Bob Prince perished in his brave attempt —or it may be that somewhere out there beyond the borders of known space he is still pursuing the enemy. But whether he ever returns or not, I can still say to you with pride this evening that such men symbolize the spirit of our race, and while they exist we shall stand against any enemy the hostile universe might send to challenge us. I offer you this message of hope, despite the dreadful and tragic destruction of the Orphelin colony. Nothing can bring back those five million wantonly destroyed lives, but I want you to join with me this evening in a solemn commitment that, together, all we people of United Earth will support any effort made by our President and the Space Corps to seek out and destroy these creatures who menace our existence. Thank you. . ." The great domed head bowed as the music surged upwards again and the scene faded.

A moment later the announcer's voice again: "And now, friends, we bring you a special report on the agricultural prospects of the Dergan Two colony, which has been forging ahead in so. . ."

The sound and picture died as Fong flipped the switch.

"Now, Commander, I believe you had some questions you wished to ask me?" he said blandly.

"Mr. President, I just don't understand," Bruce said. "You yourself have deliberately made no statement about the Orphelin massacre, and yet you allow Niebohr, who, I am ninety percent sure, was responsible for the whole thing, to blanket the entire system with this elaborate structure of hypocritical lies."

"Ninety percent certain on the evidence, or because of your own prejudice against Niebohr?"

"Mr. President—" began Bruce angrily, but the other cut him short.

"All right, Tom—I know you're sincere in your convictions," he said soothingly. "But those are the kinds of questions you would have to face if the matter were ever brought to trial, make no mistake about that. Niebohr would have the finest and the dirtiest-punching legal talent in the profession working for him, and it would be a no-holds-barred contest. He would make sure that even if he lost there would be sufficient mud thrown around to ruin everybody involved—particularly yourself."

"Is that an argument for letting him get away with this monstrous thing?" Bruce said.

"It's one of them," Fong said. "Just think for a moment. If he were found guilty and convicted, what punishment could possibly fit such a crime? If we resorted to the barbarity of capital punishment, could even that be considered a fair price—one life for those of five million people?"

"And the alternative?"

"The Space Corps Appropriations Bill comes up next week in the Senate," said Fong. "As you know, Detweiler and his isolationist hangers-on have been giving us a tough time all through the debating stages. Until this evening there was a real chance that they might succeed in killing the bill and pressing their amendments, which call for a drastic cut-back in Corps spending. However, after Niebohr's broadcast I doubt whether even Detweiler will be able to convince himself—and certainly not the people he represents—that United Earth can afford to economize in anything connected with the defense of our people against Kilroy attacks."

"Even though you and I know that there was no Kilroy attack on Orphelin Three?"

"My dear Tom, from the political point of view that makes no difference," Fong said mildly. "Nothing will bring those slaughtered people back to life—but if that vote goes through they will not have died entirely in vain."

"And Robert Prince?"

"Will remain a long-remembered hero—a symbol of self-sacrifice and bravery."

"Even though he probably died with a knife in his back."

Fong spread his pale hands. "And would it do any good to say so? To say that he died like a dog rather than that he went out in a blaze of heroic glory? Mankind has always needed its heroes in the past— and it will again in the future, make no mistake about that."

"And Niebohr?"

"You heard yourself the new position he has adopted with regard to the Corps. The weight of his influence can be a great power for good in such matters," said Fong. "As for his reasons for destroying the Orphelin Three colony—if he was indeed responsible—we may never know what they were unless he chooses to tell us."

Bruce shook his head. "I'm sorry, Mr. President, but to me the whole thing seems cynical and immoral."

"Which is precisely why you are a good Corpsman, and I am a good politician," Fong said.

Chapter Twenty-seven

*The greater the gravity of the crime, the
more it will tend to punish the innermost soul
of the criminal.*

> The Wit and Wisdom
> of Henry Fong (p. 184)

If only she were here now the moment would be
perfect, reflected Elkan Niebohr. He was standing by
the glass wall of his office at the top of the Excelsior
Building, the only illumination in the room behind
him a single desk lamp. Below him stretched the lights
of Lake Cities, and above, the stars. Out there, on
half a hundred planets colonists were working and
building, producing wealth and power for the Excelsior Colonization Corporation—for him, and for the
one who would come after him.

The decision to cut his losses on the Orphelin Three
deal had not been easy, but he was sure that it had
in the long run been the right one. Power, and the
continuity of power, had to be preserved at all costs.
Beside the protection of power, any petty considerations of sentimentality or personal preference were un-

important. People were, after all, expendable. There were so many of them. Kill off five million on one planet and within less than a week the birth-rate of the home planets alone would replace that number. People *en masse* were like ants. It seemed to him that only in a few special individuals who had fought their way to, or been born to, power was there something truly different and superior about human beings. . .

The sound of the elevator broke in on his thoughts and he turned to face the door of the outer office as Elsa entered the room. She was wearing a figure-hugging white trouser suit trimmed with gold, with a large shoulder bag of the same color. Her dark hair was swept up away from a face that had the lines of a solemn, beautiful mask.

"Baby!" he said. "I'm so pleased you came. Did you watch the show?"

"Yes, Poppa—I saw your performance," she said, moving silently across the carpet towards him.

There was something about the tone of her voice that warned him even before he saw the gun.

"Baby—what are you doing?" He stared at her in astonishment.

"I could have sold you out, Poppa," she said quietly. "This afternoon, when Tom Bruce came to me with his version of what happened in the Orphelin system, it would have been so easy for me to have told him the one thing he wanted to know. . . But I didn't. . . Maybe because I couldn't believe that even you would be so obsessed by your paranoid drive for power as to forget something I'd told you a hundred times and more."

"Baby, I don't understand." He raised one large hand in a curiously ineffectual gesture.

"No, Poppa, you don't and you never will, because in the long run people, any people, just don't count," she said. "You destroyed my mother. Admittedly she was a weak, spoiled woman, but if she hadn't become involved with a monster like you she might have lived a reasonably happy and useful life. As for my brothers, you taught the older to hate everything you stand for, and the younger how to destroy himself. You're a moral leper, contaminating everything you touch."

"For you, baby. I've tried to do everything, to give you everything you wanted and hoped for—"

"But you never listened—so how could you know?" she said harshly. "I told you that I wanted—that I needed Bob Prince."

"That's ridiculous!" he protested. "You must have had more men than the Whore of Babylon. What could one matter to you?"

"You really don't know, do you?" She was just over a meter away now. The mask was transformed into one of savage wide-eyed anger as she stared at him. "I warned you, and still you couldn't see it—because nothing could pierce the shell of your paranoia. You never cared for anyone or anybody but yourself, and so you had Bob Prince killed. . ." She raised the weapon.

"No, baby, you don't understand."

She shook her head contemptuously. "Yes I do—there's too much of you, God help me, inside my head for me not to know just how you work, to know just the kind of corruption that makes you run, and makes you completely incapable of comprehending the way I felt about Bob Prince. He was the one good, clean thing in my life, and you destroyed him. Now I'm going to destroy you."

It came to him at last that against all reason she was determined. He launched himself forward, grabbing desperately for the wrist of the hand that held the gun, but his movements were too ponderous and clumsy.

She twisted lithely away from his grasp and retreated across the heavy carpet. She raised the gun, taking steady, sure aim.

"No, baby!" he cried, "no, I don't believe it! You can't do this!"

She fired, the gun making a tiny noise, less, it seemed, than a cork popping. A needle whipped past him, splintering the panelling less than ten centimeters from his head.

Niebohr recoiled, suddenly afraid.

"Elsa, you don't know what you're doing! Listen, I had no option. You must see that. We've always understood each other; we're two of a kind, two. . ."

"That shot missed because I meant it to," she said. "The next is the one with your name on it."

"Your name too, remember!"

"Yes, this is Niebohr talking to Niebohr, Poppa. And I say that you've made the unforgivable mistake. You've no line of retreat, and—" she raised her voice in sharp but controlled anger "—and you've been found out. You didn't listen. You didn't *ever* listen, and you took what was mine. Now I take what is yours."

The needle struck Elkan Niebohr in the middle of his broad forehead. He swayed for a moment, unseeing eyes wide in the great, beaked face; then stiff as a felled tree he toppled forward to the carpet.

Elsa surveyed her handiwork, aware of a certain sense of anti-climax. It had been too easy, and too quick. . . She had not killed before, and she doubted if she would do so again. In the future there would be others to do such work for her. But this once, at least, she had expected to feel something. . .

She wiped the gun and placed it in the still-warm grasp of her victim. Then she moved to the desk and pressed the call button of the vid.

"Get me President Fong. Yes, *the* President Fong. . . I don't care what time it is, or where he is—get him!"

Waiting, she relaxed back in the big chair—*her* chair now, because now she was the Excelsior Corporation, not he. And she was so much better armed in many ways than he had been. Henry Fong might be privately sceptical about the story of her father's suicide, but he was far too practical a man to reject her offer of cooperation in the future. Everything would be arranged. She glanced out of the window at the stars, the only witnesses of what had really happened on this night. For the time being, at least, they remained neutral.

SELECTIONS FROM THE PUBLISHER
OF THE BEST SCIENCE FICTION
IN THE WORLD

SPRING 1973

*Soon to be available

To order by mail, send $1.25 per book plus 10¢
for handling to Dept. CS, Ballantine Books, 36
West 20th Street, New York, N.Y. 10003

1972 SELECTIONS FROM
THE PUBLISHER OF THE BEST
SCIENCE FICTION IN THE WORLD

TIME'S LAST GIFT	$.95
Philip José Farmer	
FIRST PERSON, PECULIAR	$.95
T. L. Sherred	
SEED OF STARS	$.95
Dan Morgan and	
John Kippax	
THE TAR-AIYM KRANG	$.95
Alan Dean Foster	
THE REALITY TRIP AND	
OTHER IMPLAUSIBILITIES	$.95
Robert Silverberg	
STARFLIGHT 3000	$.95
R. M. Mackelworth	
THE GOLD AT THE	
STARBOW'S END	$1.25
Frederik Pohl	
LIFEBOAT	$1.25
James White	

ALPHA 3	$1.25
Robert Silverberg, editor	
WHEN HARLIE WAS ONE	$1.25
David Gerrold	
WOLFWINTER	$1.25
Thomas Burnett Swann	
ALPH	$1.25
Charles Eric Maine	
THE RESURRECTION OF	
ROGER DIMENT	$.95
Douglas R. Mason	
TIMETRACKS	$.95
Keith Laumer	
SPACE SKIMMER	$.95
David Gerrold	
WITH A FINGER IN MY I	$.95
David Gerrold	
THE BEST SCIENCE FICTION	
OF THE YEAR	$1.25
Terry Carr, editor	

To order by mail, send price of book plus 10¢
for mailing to Dept. CS, Ballantine Books, 36
West 20th Street, New York, N.Y. 10003